Using EXCEL® in the Workplace

Real-world Spreadsheet Solutions to Everyday Business Problems

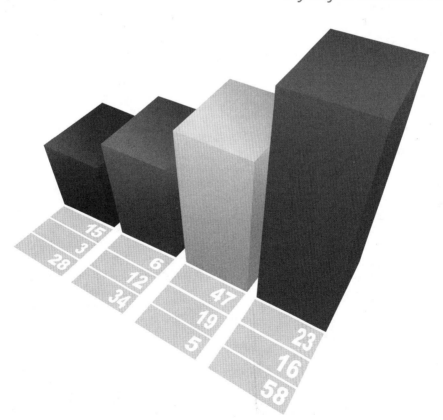

Using EXCEL® in the Workplace

Real-world Spreadsheet Solutions to Everyday Business Problems

John Kamper

SkillPath® Publications

Editor: Bill Cowles

Technical Reviewers: Jeff Martin and David Codrington

Cover design: Jason Dill

Layout: Danielle Horn

ISBN: 978-1-934589-38-0

Printed in the United States of America

Table of Contents

Introduction

Using Excel® in the Workplace demonstrates easy and simple ways to get needed information from the spreadsheets you create and/or work with in your everyday business life. It's not only about how to use spreadsheet software—it's about how you can use spreadsheets of any kind to be more productive and effective.

While the discussion and examples used in this book are based on Microsoft® Excel®, if you can enter numbers and text in cells you can use the techniques in this book. There is no such thing as basic or advanced here, just useful.

Most people learn Microsoft® Excel® by starting out with the "basics." What toolbars are, what the various buttons do, how to enter numbers and text, what a formula is, how to format cells and some fundamental functions such as "AutoSum." These formulas and functions are the tools Excel® provides to extract the information you want from the worksheets. You build powerful spreadsheets that provide the information you need by using these basic tools.

But just because the "basics" provide the information you need doesn't mean they are the easiest way to harvest the information from your worksheets.

That could be because many think the word "basic" means "easy" and the word "advanced" means "difficult." In many instances, it's just the opposite. Many of the so-called "advanced" topics in Excel® are easier to use, save you time and work and provide more information than if you just stick to the "basics."

Excel® contains literally thousands of ways to gather information. It provides a wide spectrum of tools for every situation. Many of them are for advanced mathematical, statistical and scientific purposes that the everyday user needs only on occasion. *Using Excel® in the Workplace* doesn't attempt to cover everything, just those situations that most business people encounter in their everyday workplace.

The real world—your workplace—presents problems you have to analyze in order to solve. These are the word problems, if you will, that many avoided in school. In the typical workplace, there's no one to explain how to get the information you need to solve the problem. Once you have the data, it's up to you to analyze the situation and come up with the solution. You then have to figure out which tools to use to get the information you want. The "how to" comes after the "what do I want?"

Using Excel® in the Workplace starts with the premise that you are familiar with basic Windows®—how to open a program, how to cut/copy/paste, how to save and open files, basic file management, what toolbars are, working with dialog boxes, etc. I encourage you to experiment with the different options in dialog boxes and dig further into the elements that you use the most. Make Excel® your own.

Get the most from this book

In order to get the most from this book, apply the examples provided to your own situation. The examples in the following chapters, taken from a mortgage lender's workplace, are just that—examples. Are you in management? Sales? Inventory control? Human resources? Accounting? Are you an administrative assistant? When you see the word "loan" think "sales," or whatever you are tracking. When you see the word "processor" think "sales support," etc.

Relate the Situations sections of the examples to the situations that arise in your workplace. What use can you make of them in your job? It's up to you to take the examples in the book, find the parallels in your own situations and adapt them to come up with your own solutions.

Conventions and useful information

A few explanations to help you as you go through the book:

- The ">" symbol, when used in an example such as "Click Open > TAB," means "Click on the Open menu item, then press TAB"

- The instruction "Type" precedes words in a different font. You are to type those words or symbols. Example: Type `Sales Rep`.

- "Data" is what you enter into a cell

- "Information" is what you get from data

- The "active" cell is the cell you enter data into

Cursor shapes and uses

Depending on where you point your cursor, it takes on different shapes. The following are the most common shapes you will use.

Name	Shape	Purpose
White Cross		Selects the active cell; click and drag to select more cells
White Arrow		Selects items from the menus
Black Cross		AutoFill tool—copies formulas using relative referencing
4-headed Arrow		Used to move charts and graphics
Corner Shape		Indicates cell ready for more data; use as AutoFill tool before pressing ENTER
Insertion Point (I Beam)		Blinking bar that indicates where data will be entered. Appears in active cell or Formula bar.
Sizing Arrow		Sizes charts and graphics

Excel® 2003 shortcuts

The CTRL key + letters:

- **CTRL + A:** Selects a range or the entire worksheet
- **CTRL + B:** Makes the cell and its contents bold
- **CTRL + C:** Copies selected data
- **CTRL + F:** Finds search items
- **CTRL + G:** Moves the active cell to a specific cell
- **CTRL + H:** Replaces specific data with desired data
- **CTRL + I:** Italicizes cell and its contents
- **CTRL + N:** Opens a new workbook
- **CTRL + O:** Opens an existing workbook
- **CTRL + P:** Prints the worksheet
- **CTRL + S:** Saves the workbook
- **CTRL + U:** Underlines the cell and its contents
- **CTRL + V:** Pastes selected data
- **CTRL + W:** Closes a workbook
- **CTRL + X:** Cuts (moves) selected data
- **CTRL + Y:** Repeats actions
- **CTRL + Z:** Undoes actions

Function key shortcuts:

- **F1:** Help
- **F2:** Edit active cell
- **F7:** Spell check
- **F11:** With data selected, automatically creates a chart on new worksheet
- **F12:** Save As

Selection commands

- The Active Cell: The active cell is selected by default

To select all, or the entire worksheet:

- Keyboard: CTRL + A
- Mouse: Click the "Select All" button, the blank button at the upper left, where rows and columns meet

To select more than one cell:

- Click and drag across the cells you want to select
- Click one cell, press the SHIFT key, click another cell—the entire range between the cells is selected
- Click one cell, press the CTRL key, click other separated cells—allows you to select individual cells

To select a column:

- Keyboard: CTRL + SPACE—selects the column that contains the active cell
- Mouse: Click a column header

To select a row:

- Keyboard: SHIFT + SPACE key
- Mouse: Click row number

To select a contiguous range:

- Keyboard: From the active cell press the SHIFT key, press the arrow keys to extend the selection in any direction
- Keyboard and Mouse: From the active cell, press the SHIFT key, click the last cell in the range you want to select
- Mouse: Click and drag across desired cells

To select separated cells:

- Mouse: From the active cell, press the CTRL key and click the cells you want to select

Navigation keys

- **CTRL + PAGE UP, CTRL + PAGE DOWN:** Moves between worksheets
- **TAB:** Advances the active cell to the right
- **SHIFT + TAB:** Moves the active cell to the left
- **PAGE UP:** Moves the active cell up one screen
- **PAGE DOWN:** Moves the active cell down one screen
- **HOME:** Moves the active cell to Column A in the same row
- **CTRL + HOME:** Returns the active cell to Cell A1
- **CTRL + any arrow key:** Moves the active cell to the last cell in a row or column that contains data
- **CTRL + END:** Moves the active cell to the last cell in the working range
- **CTRL + G:** Moves the active cell to a specific cell

Default cell alignment

- Numbers are aligned to the right of a cell
- Text is aligned to the left of a cell

If the text is too wide for the cell to contain, it will extend over the cell(s) to the right, if empty. If there is data in the cell(s) to the right, the text is truncated. You have to widen the column to see the entire contents.

If a number is too wide for the cell, ##### signs appear in the cell. To see the number, widen the column.

You might see a number with scientific notation such as "5.64E = 11." To see the number itself, click the Comma Style button on the Formatting toolbar.

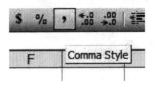

Bonus—Financial Statement Analysis Template

Included on the accompanying CD is a workbook named *Financial Analysis Template.xlt*.

It provides built-in formulas to help you easily analyze financial statements. Simply type in the numbers from you Balance Sheet and Income Statement and the ratios are automatically calculated for you. You have to supply the title information, date, formatting, insert rows, etc. to match your company's requirements. More information is provided in the template.

Note: It is a template. You will have to change the name to save your workbook.

Good luck and success in all that you do!

Chapter One

Design Your Worksheet

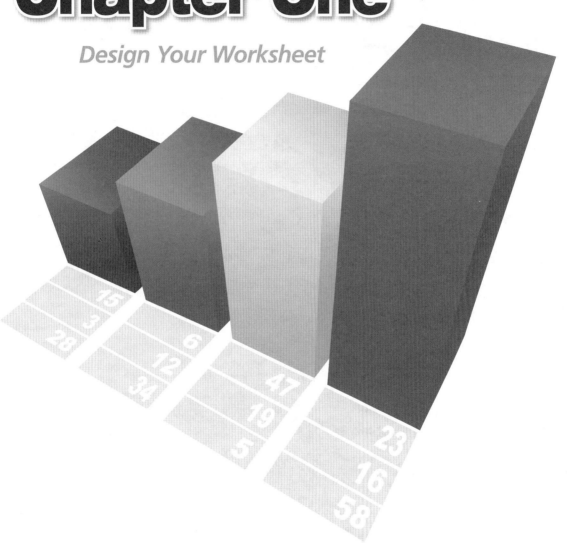

Begin with the end in mind

Excel® is different from most programs. The purpose of a word processing program, Microsoft® Word, for example, is to create and store data. It is static information. It sits on a page. You can retrieve it and read it, but you get out only what you put in. Excel®'s purpose is different.

In Excel®, you put data in to get information out. You input the hard data you already have to get information about that data. You want Excel® to add, subtract, multiply, divide and contort that data in any number of ways so you can get out of it all the information it contains.

The first thing to consider when starting a worksheet, then, is the information you want to get out of the hard data you put in it.

Information needs vary from job to job. Do you want totals of numbers? Are you tracking inventory? Do you use statistics? Are you a mathematician? A scientist? A salesperson? How are you tracking that information—by hour, day, week, month, quarter, year-to-date? The industry you work in, your job and the different kinds of data you track determine how you design your worksheet.

The information you want to get out determines the layout of the rows and columns—your design. This takes some planning. For example, do you want to track "sales by month" or "sales by sales rep"? The way you lay out your spreadsheet is often just as important as the data you input. What information do you want in columns? What information do you want in rows? Where on the spreadsheet do you want that information?

Another important consideration is: "Who reads the reports you prepare?" Are they for your eyes only, or do you prepare the reports for someone else?

It's one thing if they're for yourself and most of the time you just read them off your monitor. In that situation you don't particularly have to be concerned about their appearance or formatting. You know what and where the information is and you don't have to worry about how it appears.

It's entirely different if you prepare the reports for your clients or your boss, who might pass them on to senior management. Designing for your audience is essential to preparing effective reports. Your reports not only provide meaningful—if not essential—information. They are a reflection of your professionalism, knowledge and skill.

An incomplete report, a report that has errors or a report that looks unprofessional will affect the confidence people put in you and your work. Your ability to use Excel® to analyze situations, create solutions and provide meaningful information has dual benefits. It not only provides that information, but it also reflects your competence and potential for advancement. It has an effect on your salary, potential raises and position within your company.

Situation:

You work for My Mortgage Company, a company that originates real estate loans. You work in the Single Family Loan department. You are a loan representative, the equivalent of a sales representative in a different industry. Your primary responsibility is to generate first mortgages for single family homes.

Your company is expanding the Second Mortgage Loan department, another department your boss manages. He has asked you to prepare a sales report for the Second Mortgage Loan department. He wants to know which months/quarters produce the most second mortgages.

Every company has a business cycle. More sales occur in some months, fewer in others. Management needs this information for staffing, advertising, budgeting, expansion potential and other business considerations.

Your boss has been asked to report on the loan production cycle for second mortgages. He wants to know which quarter and month produce the largest amount of loans closed, which month has the least and the average loan amount. Your boss asks you to prepare the report.

He gives you the sales data for second mortgages for the year 2007. He leaves the design of the report up to you, but wants it entitled "Second Mortgage Report 2007."

He doesn't mention it, but you know he will use your information in his report to senior management.

Design a sales report. You want the information to appear in the right place with the correct emphasis. You have to decide which tools to use to get the information and how to do it in the easiest way.

Your first consideration is: What information do you want to get out of the report? The primary purpose of the report is to list the volume of loans by month and quarter. The secondary requirement is to provide information about the sales reps, ranking the size of their loans and their loan production.

Your second consideration is: Who will read the report? Because it's quite likely that your report will be shared with upper management, you want to make it stand out, both in the information it provides and in its appearance. Because it will reflect your abilities, you spend some time thinking about it. What will be the best layout to provide the necessary information? You come up with the following tentative design (see the workbook *Tentative Layout.xls* on the accompanying CD).

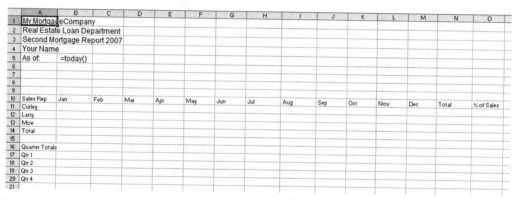

Features: The Fill Handle, AutoFill, Relative Referencing, Custom Lists

Step 1

After typing the report title information and the sales reps' names, you use the Fill Handle and AutoFill (very useful tools in Excel®) to list the months. The Fill Handle and AutoFill are tools that fill out the months of the year, the days of the week, the quarters of the year, etc., without your having to type each item in the list.

To enter the months:

- Click on cell B10

- Type Jan (you can also type the full word—January instead of Jan, Monday instead of Mon, Quarter instead of Qtr, etc.)

- To enter the month without advancing the active cell, click the green checkmark to the left of the *fx* button on the Formula toolbar. This allows you to use the Fill tool without repositioning the active cell rather than pressing ENTER, the TAB key or the right arrow.

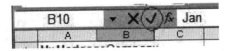

Step 2

To enter the remaining months, use the Fill Handle and AutoFill.

The Fill Handle is the small square on the lower right corner of the cell or selected range.

AutoFill fills in the remaining months.

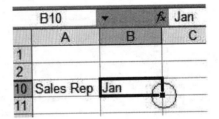

AutoFill allows you to copy the data/formulas/functions/custom lists to other cells, changing the data, etc. to correspond to the appropriate cells.

- Hover the white arrow over the Fill Handle until it changes to a small black cross: ✚ (refer to the Cursor Shapes Table in the Introduction)

- Click and drag the black cross to the right to fill in the months of the year

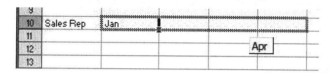

To create a custom list:

Step 1

- Click Tools > Options > the Custom Lists tab

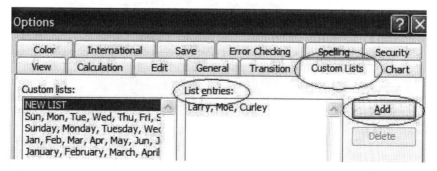

The Custom Lists box shows the existing lists. The default lists are the days of the week, the months of the year and quarters—both spelled out and abbreviated.

Step 2

- Click in the List Entries text box

- Type the names of the reps—Larry, Moe and Curley—separated by commas (you can either separate the names with a comma or press ENTER to place each name in a separate cell)

- Click the Add button > OK

Step 3

- Click Cell All

- Type Larry

Hint:

Before you press ENTER, look at the Fill Handle. It takes the shape of a corner shape, such as you might use to hold a photograph in place in a scrapbook (refer to the Cursor Shapes Table in the Introduction). You can use this for AutoFill as well.

- Hover the cursor over the corner shape until the Fill Handle appears and drag down. The sales reps' names are entered.

- Click on cell A17 and use the same procedure to enter the quarters. Your tentative worksheet appears as follows:

	A20	▼	fx Qtr 4		
	A	B	C	D	E
1	My MortgageCompany				
2	Real Estate Loan Department				
3	Second Mortgage Report 2007				
9					
10	Sales Rep	Jan	Feb	Mar	Apr
11	Curley				
12	Larry				
13	Moe				
14	Total				
15					
16	Quarter Totals				
17	Qtr 1				
18	Qtr 2				
19	Qtr 3				
20	Qtr 4				
21					

Step 4

- Check the design

Hint:

Don't waste time by inputting all your data before you check the design. Take time to evaluate the design before you go too far.

When you inspect the results, you see that this layout is too wide—it scrolls off the right side of the page. (Open the file *Tentative Layout.xls* on the accompanying CD to see the layout so far.)

Situation:

After you've inserted the Months, Total and % of Sales headers, you see that the columns go out to column O, too far to print on one page. You want it to be on one page for ease of use. Also, all the information is at the top of the page, which leaves the bottom part of the pages blank. This layout is unsatisfactory.

Solution:

You want to see if changing the design to have the monthly loan figures in the columns and the sales reps numbers in the rows would be better. You transpose the rows and columns.

Features: Paste Special, Transpose row/columns, the =TODAY() function and Split screen

Step 1

- Click cell A10
- Press the CTRL key, the SHIFT key and the END key all at the same time. This automatically selects the working range, cells A10 to O20.
- Copy the selection

Step 2

- Click cell A25 > Edit > Paste Special > the Transpose box. This allows you to compare both layouts.

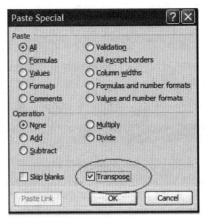

The months are now in rows and the sales reps in columns. (If you followed along, open the workbook *Tentative Layout 2.xls*.)

	A	B	C	D
1	My MortgageCompany			
2	Real Estate Loan Department			
3	Second Mortgage Report 2007			
4	Your Name			
5	As of:	=today()		
6				
25	Sales Rep	Larry	Moe	Curley
26	Jan			
27	Feb			
28	Mar			
29	Apr			
30	May			
31	Jun			
32	Jul			
33	Aug			
34	Sep			
35	Oct			
36	Nov			
37	Dec			
38	Total			
39	% of Sales			
40				
41				

This design would make the report easy to format, print and distribute and it keeps all the information on one page, but it is not satisfactory.

Your boss's primary goal is to know the loan production by quarter and month. This design makes the sales reps' performance the primary information and the monthly sales information the secondary. It's just the opposite of what you want.

Also, in order to call attention to the primary information, you decide to include a Summary Section toward the top of the worksheet, so it stands out and management can easily refer to the primary information.

You redesign the report as follows. (Open the workbook *Final Layout.xls* on the accompanying CD.)

	A1		*fx* My MortgageCompany		
	A	B	C	D	E
1	My MortgageCompany				
2	Real Estate Loan Department				
3	Second Mortgage Report 2007				
4	Your Name				
5	As of:	=Today()			
6					
7					
8	Summary by:	Quarter		Summary by:	Month
9	Largest			Largest	
10	Smallest			Smallest	
11	Average			Average	
12					
13					
14					
15	Month	Curley	Larry	Moe	Total
16	Jan				
17	Feb				
18	Mar				
19	Qtr 1 Totals				
20					

Hint:

Notice the function "=TODAY()" in cell B5. Because you want the date to always show the current date—the date the worksheet is opened—you typed that function. It always displays the date the worksheet is opened. If you want the date of the report to remain the same, type the date in any format you please.

The example contains only a few records (rows). When the data you enter flows down into many rows, you often cannot see the column headers. Use the Split Screen feature to hide intervening rows.

- Click below the row that you want to remain visible. For example, in the workbook *Final Layout.xls*, click cell A6.

- Click Window > Split

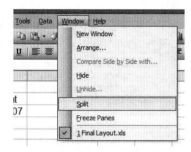

This inserts a beige line across the columns. As you enter more records, row 5 always remains visible. (To remove the split, click Window > Remove Split.)

	A	B	C	D	E
1	My MortgageCompany				
2	Real Estate Loan Department				
3	Second Mortgage Report 2007				
4	Your Name				
5	As of:	=Today()			
6					
7					
8	Summary by:	Quarter		Summary by:	Month
9	Largest			Largest	
10	Smallest			Smallest	
11	Average			Average	
12					

Results

You've finished creating the best design for the report and its intended audience. It locates the important information at the top, where it is most visible. The secondary information is detailed below it. It fits on one page, provides the required information in an easy-to-read print and fills the page better. You decide to use it.

Chapter Two

Create a Sales Report

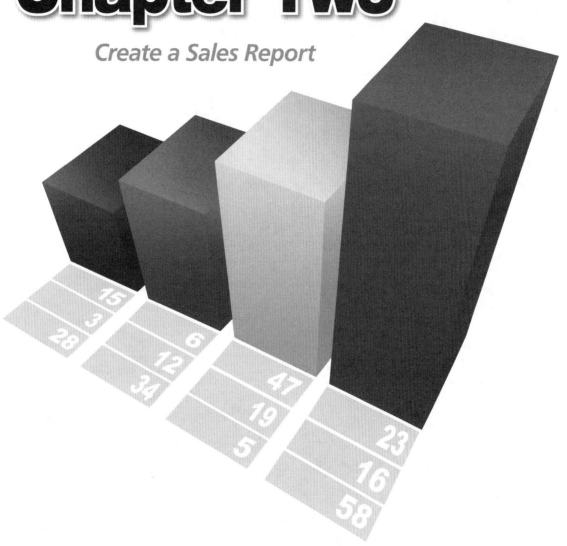

Who sold the most, when?

You have finalized the design for your report. You know where you want the data to appear. You now have to input it.

You want to enter a series of numbers or text into the appropriate cells as easily as possible. You normally use ENTER, TAB or the arrow keys to move from cell to cell. This has a disadvantage when you have entered the data in the last cell of a row or column. You have to stop typing, pick up the mouse and click on the first cell in the next line or row to enter data there. You want an easier way.

Solution:

Enter the data into cells you have already selected. (Refer to the Introduction for the different methods of selecting cells.)

Feature: Selection for data entry (To follow along, open the workbook *Select cells.xls* from the accompanying CD.)

Step 1

Select the range of cells into which you want to enter the information before you enter data:

- Select cells C16 through E18

	A	B	C	D	E	F
1	My MortgageCompany					
2	Real Estate Loan Department					
3	Second Mortgage Report 2007					
4	Your name					
5	As of:	=TODAY()				
10		Summary by:	Quarter		Summary by:	Month
11		Largest			Largest	
12		Smallest			Smallest	
13		Average			Average	
14						
15	Qtr 1	Rep	Jan	Feb	Mar	Qtr 1 Total
16		Larry				
17		Moe				
18		Curley				
19		Total				

The cell with the white background is the active cell. Start entering data here and move from cell to cell using the TAB or ENTER keys. With these cells selected, when you reach the last cell of a row or column and press TAB or ENTER, the active cell automatically moves to the first cell in the next selected row or column.

Step 2

- Type the loan information from cell to cell horizontally (TAB) or vertically (ENTER)
- Use the same procedure to enter the loan data for the remaining months of the year (To follow along, open file *Monthly numbers.xls* from the accompanying CD. It has the monthly sales added in the appropriate cells.)

Situation:

Now that you have entered the loan information, you have to total the sales for each month by each sales rep.

Solution:

Create formulas to find the monthly totals.

Features: Formulas and Functions

Formulas are equations that you create for a specific circumstance. Every formula begins with an equal sign: "=."

Excel® provides many formulas for you to use, called "Functions." To find out just how many there are:

- Click Insert > Function
- Scroll through the list of functions under the All selection—there are over two hundred of them. The dialog box provides an explanation of each function as you click on it.

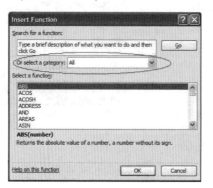

In arithmetic, you call a formula an "algebraic expression": add, subtract, multiply or divide, among others. These are called operators. The keys for these operators are the + – * / keys, found both on the alpha keyboard and the ten-key number pad.

When computing formulas, Excel® first multiplies or divides, then adds and subtracts. Excel® interprets the formula "=7+6*2" as "multiply 6 times 2, then add 7 to that result to come up with the answer 19." To have Excel® first add 7 and 6 and then multiply by 2 to come up with the answer "26," put parentheses around the "7+6" to read as follows: "=(7+6)*2."

Hint:

When referring to numbers in cells, rather than retyping the data in the cell, you can simply click on the cell that holds that data. If the data in that cell changes, the formula changes accordingly.

Step 1

Create the formula to add the monthly loan production for January. In the *Monthly numbers.xls* workbook:

- Click cell C19
- Type =
- Click cell C16
- Type +
- Click cell C17
- Type +
- Click cell C18
- Press ENTER

The total sales for the month of January are displayed in cell C19 as "465000." The Formula bar shows what's really in the cell:

Arial	10	**B** *I* U	≡ ≡ ≡
C19	▼	*fx* =C16+C17+C18	

	A	B	C	
1	My MortgageCompany			
15	Qtr 1	Rep	Jan	Feb
16		Larry	150000	
17		Moe	155000	
18		Curley	160000	
19		Total	465000	
20				

Step 2

Once you have the formula for the month of January, you want to easily and quickly create the formulas for the remaining months.

Copy the formula using AutoFill to get the totals for the other months (this is the same procedure you used to input the months of the year and the Custom List entries). AutoFill copies and changes the formulas so the cell references are relative and appropriate to the column or row you copy.

- Hover the cursor over the AutoFill square until it changes to a black cross

- Click and drag to cells D19 and E19. This copies and changes the formula to sum the sales for the months of January, February and March.

- After you've copied it, the formula to cell D19 reads "=D16+D17+D18"

- In E19, the formula reads "=E16+E17+E18"

- The formulas have been copied, and they reflect the relative (appropriate) position of the cells

Step 3

Using the same procedure, enter the formulas for the Quarter 1 Totals in cells F16 through F20.

This procedure is time consuming and requires a number of actions to enter all the formulas. You want to use a faster way.

Create a formula with a double-click.

Features: AutoSum and Relative Copying

The AutoSum tool is an even simpler and faster way to total rows or columns. The AutoSum button uses the Sum Function to calculate totals.

Step 1

- Click on cell C27
- Click the AutoSum button on the standard toolbar

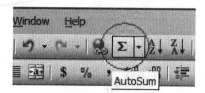

The AutoSum tool selects the cells immediately above the active cell (if adding numbers in columns) or immediately to its left (if adding rows).

	B	C	
	eCompany		
	Rep	Apr	May
	Larry	165000	
	Moe	170000	
	Curley	225000	
	Total	=SUM(C24:C26)	

Step 2

- Click the AutoSum button a second time and the result of the formula is entered

In short, you simply double-click the AutoSum button to create the formula. The function reads: "=SUM(C24:C26)." In words it reads, "Sum the numbers in cells C24 through C26."

- Copy this formula using the AutoFill button as well to cells D27 and E27
- Click on cell F24 and create the formulas for the Quarter 2 Totals

Hint:

You used the Fill Handle/AutoFill tool to insert the months and quarters and to create a Custom List. You also use it to copy formulas. It copies them using Relative Copying. Relative Copying allows you to copy formulas from one cell to another, automatically changing the cell reference numbers relative to the rows or columns where you paste the formula. It saves you the time/mistakes of creating new formulas for each cell. You can use any of the operators to create the formula needed. An example might be "=SUM(Z24 - Z25)." This means "subtract cell Z25 from cell Z24."

Hint:

Be careful. The AutoSum button stops selecting cells, either vertically or horizontally, when it reaches an empty cell. You can click and drag the cells you want to add, if a blank cell happens to be interspersed. In the following example, notice the range selected includes the blank cell.

	15
	20
	25
	30
Total:	=SUM(K10:K14)

This still takes too many actions. You want to total the sales by both row and column in one step.

Use the AutoSum tool to add both rows and columns.

Step 1

Select the cells with the data in them, the empty row for the month totals plus the empty column for the Quarter 3 totals:

- Click cell C32

- Hold the SHIFT key down

- Click cell F35

	A	B	C	D	E	F
1	My MortgageCompany					
2	Real Estate Loan Department					
30						
31	Qtr 3	Rep	Jul	Aug	Sep	Qtr 3 Total
32		Larry	250000	400000	500000	
33		Moe	155000	250000	450000	
34		Curley	155000	155000	125000	
35		Total				
36						

Step 2

- Click the AutoSum button. The totals are automatically entered.

C32		f_x	250000			
	A	B	C	D	E	F
1	My MortgageCompany					
2	Real Estate Loan Department					
30						
31	Qtr 3	Rep	Jul	Aug	Sep	Qtr 3 Total
32		Larry	250000	400000	500000	1150000
33		Moe	155000	250000	450000	855000
34		Curley	155000	155000	125000	435000
35		Total	560000	805000	1075000	2440000
36						

Use any of the above methods to create the formulas for the totals for Quarter 4.

Now that you have the totals for the months and quarters, you need to enter the formulas for the YTD totals.

Create the formulas.

Feature: Links. A link is simply a reference to another cell. Links can refer to cells in the same worksheet, a cell in a different worksheet in the same workbook, to a different program or even to the Web (a hyperlink).

In this situation, you merely want to reflect the totals for cells C19 through F19 in cells C21 through F21. To create the formula takes two easy steps using a link:

Step 1

- Click cell C21
- Type =
- Click C19 > ENTER (the formula in cell C21 reads "=C19")

Step 2

- Use the Fill Handle to copy the formula to cells D21 through F21

You now want to create the formulas for the YTD totals for the remaining quarters.

Create the formulas.

Step 1

- Click cell C29
- Type =
- Click cell C21
- Press +
- Click cell C27 > ENTER
- The total is entered; the formula reads: "=C21+C27"

Step 2

- Use the AutoFill handle to copy the formula to cells D29 through F29

Step 3

- Use the same procedure to create the formulas for the remaining YTD cells and copy them accordingly

The formula in:

- Cell C37 reads "=C29+C35"
- Cell C45 reads "=C37+C43"

You have completed the first requirement, to find the total sales by sales rep, month, quarter and year to date. (To compare your worksheet, open the workbook *Report with totals.xls* from the accompanying CD.) Now that you have this information, you can create the formulas for the Summary section. You have placed this at the top of the page because this information is the primary purpose of the report. It should hold a prominent position.

Solution:

Create the formulas for the Summary by Quarter section.

Features: The Function Wizard, the Functions MAX, MIN and AVERAGE. These functions are built into Excel® and are simple to use. MAX finds the largest number in a range, MIN finds the smallest, and AVERAGE averages the numbers in a range.

Step 1

Determine which quarter has produced the largest amount of loans. The quarter totals are in cells F19, F27, F35 and F43. Use the MAX function.

- Click cell C11

- Click the *fx* button—the Function Wizard—on the Formula bar

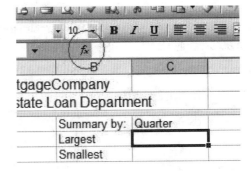

The Insert Function dialog box appears.

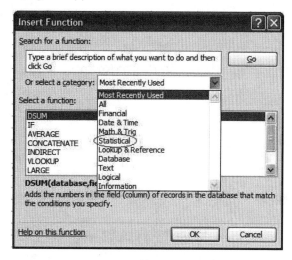

Step 2

Find the MAX function which is in the Statistical category:

- Click on the Statistical category and scroll down until you find MAX (it may also appear in the Most Recently Used category)

- Press ENTER, or click OK

- The Function Arguments box appears

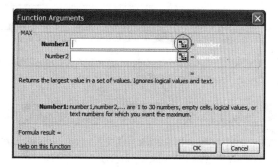

Hint:

You can move a dialog box out of the way by clicking and dragging on its Title bar. You can also Minimize/Restore this box by clicking on the button to the right of the text box. (See the circled box in the figure above.)

Step 3

Enter the quarter totals in the appropriate boxes. The cursor is in the Number 1 box.

- Click cell F19
- Press the TAB key to move to the Number 2 box
- Click cell F27 > TAB
- Click cell F35 > TAB
- Click cell F43
- Click OK

Before clicking OK the dialog box looks like the following. Note that the total appears in the dialog box itself.

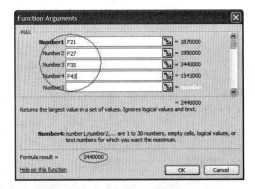

Situation:

The largest loan amount originated in any quarter in 2007 was $2,440,000. You still have to determine the smallest and average loan amounts.

Solution:

Follow the same steps as above using the Function Wizard, but use the MIN and AVERAGE functions rather than the MAX function.

The formula for the quarter with the least amount (minimum) of loan production, cell C21, is "=MIN(F19,F27,F35,F43)" resulting in $1,541,000.

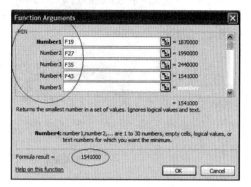

The formula for the average loan amount, cell C13, is "=AVERAGE(F19,F27,F35,F43)" resulting in $1,960,250.

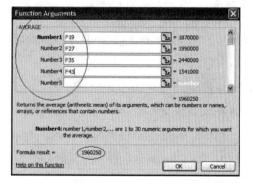

Now you have the Summary Information by Quarter. The largest loan production in any quarter is $2,440,000; the smallest is $1,541,000; the average is $1,962,250. You need similar information for the months.

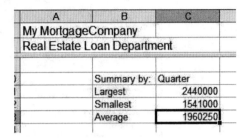

	A	B	C
	My MortgageCompany		
	Real Estate Loan Department		
		Summary by:	Quarter
		Largest	2440000
		Smallest	1541000
		Average	1960250

The formula will be the same but longer because you have to enter the cells for twelve months. The procedure is the same as for the Quarterly Summary Information, except you choose the months' totals instead of the quarter totals:

- Click cell F11

- Click the Function Wizard button and choose the MAX function

- In the Number 1 box, click cell C19 > Tab to the next box

- Use the same procedure to select the totals for all of the months

- Click OK. The formula in cell F11 is "=MAX(C19,D19,E19,C27,D27,E27,C35,D35,E35, C43,D43,E43)."

- Use the same procedure as above to create the MIN and AVERAGE functions in cells F12 and F13

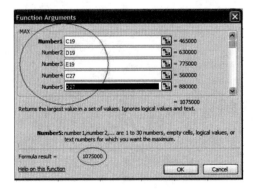

You now have the statistics for loan production by month. The largest loan production in any month is $1,075,000; smallest loan production in any month is $465,000; the average loan amount is $653,417. (If you have followed along, compare your worksheet to the worksheet *Report with summary.xls* on the accompanying CD.)

Situation:

You have the required numbers, but you haven't identified the quarter or month the numbers occurred in. Which quarter had the largest loan production? Which had the smallest, etc.? You could simply let the reviewer search for the numbers that match, but, with all the different numbers, this information would not easily be apparent. You want to point out the quarters and months to the reviewer so he or she won't have to search for them.

Solution:

Color is an easy way to catch attention. You decide to use color to match the Summary by Quarter numbers with the actual quarter numbers.

You color the background of the Summary by Quarter numbers to match the months that contain those numbers. The quarter with the largest loan production, $2,440,000, was Quarter 3, reflected in cell F35.

Features: Fill Color, Format Painter and Font Color

Step 1

Change the background color of cells C11 and F35 to identify which quarter had the most loan production.

- Select cell C8

- Click the Fill Color button and choose bright green > ENTER

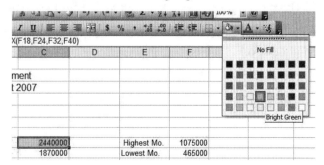

Step 2

Copy the formatting to cell F35.

- In cell C8, click the Format Painter tool once

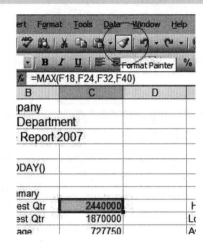

- Click on cell F35 to copy the Fill Color. Format Painter turns itself off.

Step 3

Color the background for the quarter with the lowest loan production.

- Use the procedure above to color the background of cells C9 and F18 sky blue

The average number, cell C10, doesn't correlate to any specific cell, so there's no need to highlight that cell.

You also want to identify the months to match the Summary by Months section.

Use color to match the Summary by Month numbers with the month's numbers. In this situation, you'll color the font of the Summary by Months numbers to match the month totals. The month with the highest loan production was September, reflected in cell E32.

- Select cells F8 and E32

- Click cell F8

- Press the Cᴛʀʟ key > click cell E32

- Click the Font Color button

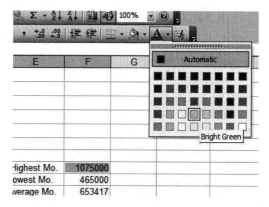

- Choose bright green. This matches the Fill Color of the highest quarter's production.

- The month with the least loan production was January

- Use the same procedure to change the Font Color of cells F9 and F16 to sky blue to reflect the month with the lowest loan production

You've changed the colors of cells to match. You need to create a Legend to explain the color coding.

Enter the Legend information, as in the following figure, by simply typing the words beginning in cell D2. Press ENTER after each segment to continue the information through D5. The text is contained in cells D2, D3, D4 and D5. Bold the cells.

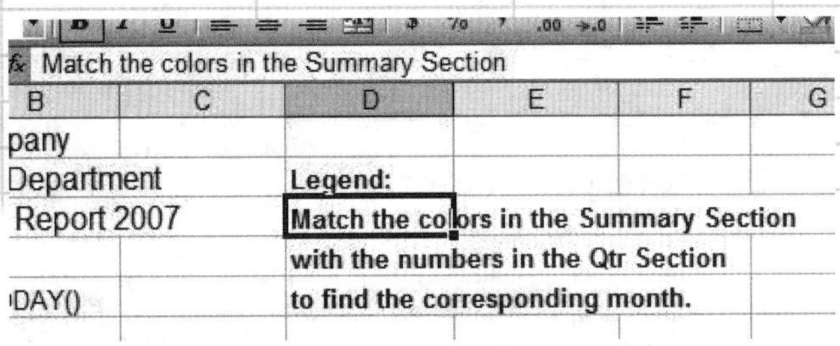

Hint:

Note that the text of the cells flows over to the cells to the right when entering text. Text flows over the cells to the right until it encounters a cell that has something in it, either text or numbers. If the cell to the right of the text has something in it, the text will be truncated. It will not show or print.

If you've followed along, your worksheet should now look like the file *Report with highlights.xls* on the accompanying CD.

You have almost completed the report. You have designed the spreadsheet so it all fits on one page. Before you do the final formatting, you want to check to see how it prints.

Preview the page on-screen rather than print it. It saves time, energy, money and the environment.

Feature: Print Preview.

- Click on the Print Preview button

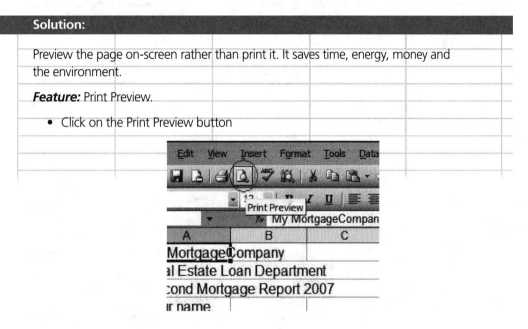

Your worksheet should look like the following figure:

My MortgageCompany
Real Estate Loan Department
Second Mortgage Report 2007
Your name
As of   =TODAY()

Legend:
Match the colors in the Summary Section
with the numbers in the Qtr Section
to find the corresponding month.

Summary				
Largest Qtr	2440000		Highest Mo.	1075000
Lowest Qtr	1870000		Lowest Mo.	465000
Average	727750		Average Mo.	653417

Qtr 1	Rep	Jan	Feb	Mar	Qtr 1 Total
	Curley	150000	200000	125000	475000
	Larry	155000	210000	200000	565000
	Moe	160000	220000	450000	830000
	Total	465000	630000	775000	1870000
	YTD Total	465000	630000	775000	1870000

Qtr 2	Rep	Apr	May	Jun	Qtr 2 Total
	Curley	165000	230000	100000	495000
	Larry	170000	300000	100000	570000
	Moe	225000	350000	350000	925000
	Total	560000	880000	550000	1990000
	YTD Total	1025000	1510000	1325000	3860000

Qtr 3	Rep	Jul	Aug	Sep	Qtr 3 Total
	Curley	250000	400000	500000	1150000
	Larry	155000	250000	450000	855000
	Moe	155000	155000	125000	435000
	Total	560000	805000	1075000	2440000
	YTD Total	1585000	2315000	2400000	6300000

Qtr 4	Rep	Oct	Nov	Dec	Qtr 4 Total
	Curley	165000	170000	116000	451000
	Larry	175000	185000	165000	525000
	Moe	185000	150000	230000	565000
	Total	525000	505000	511000	1541000
	YTD Total	2110000	2820000	2911000	7841000

You have the numbers, totals and highlights, but the report is not finished. You still have to format the report so it's easier to read. The numbers and text have no formatting. There is nothing to delineate one section of the report from another.

Format the report.

Features: AutoFormat and adjust column width/row height

If you wanted to spend a lot of time and effort, you could format each individual row/column/cell by using the Format > Cell command. In the following figure, you can see that you can format numbers in at least 12 different ways. The six tabs across the top are indications that you can format cell alignment, fonts, etc. But rather than format each element individually, you can format cells in blocks using AutoFormat.

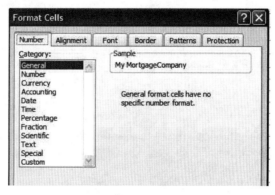

AutoFormat is a much simpler and faster way to format a worksheet. It has preset formats for text (bold, center alignment, etc.) and numbers (dollar signs and commas) as well as different color combinations and shadings to highlight different areas.

You want to have dollar signs and commas on the numbers so they will be easier to read.

You'll choose an AutoFormat style that applies that formatting.

A small but important point—your corporation uses a violet color in its logo, stationery, advertising, etc. Your report will be more professional if you can use that color in your formatting. You choose an AutoFormat style that uses a matching color.

Given the layout of your worksheet, you decide to format each section by itself to separate the different sections of the report. (If you've followed along, the file *Report with highlights.xls* from the accompanying CD is open.)

Step 1

- Select cells A1 through B5, the title area

- Click Format > AutoFormat

- Click the Accounting 2 style > OK

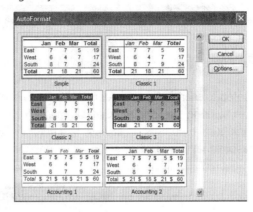

Click away from the selection to see the result. Note that AutoFormat has placed borders on some cells. Borders are the lines that delineate cells. You can place borders on all lines of a cell.

Step 2

Apply the same AutoFormat to the Summary section. You can save steps by copying the AutoFormat rather than going through the steps again.

- Select cells B7 through F10

- Click Edit > Repeat AutoFormat. Note the shortcut CTRL + Y —the shortcut key for Edit, Repeat (the last command).

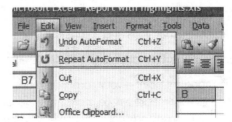

You notice that dollar signs, commas and decimals have been added to the numbers. You don't want decimals to show. If you change the decimal places now, the Repeat Command will reduce decimals, not apply the AutoFormat. You wait until later to fix this problem.

Step 3

- Use the same technique to apply the AutoFormat to the Quarter 1 area, cells B12 through F18

Situation:

As you apply the AutoFormat, you find that you can't see all the sections in the worksheet.

Solution:

Change the scale of the worksheet so that you can see all the rows.

Feature: The Zoom button

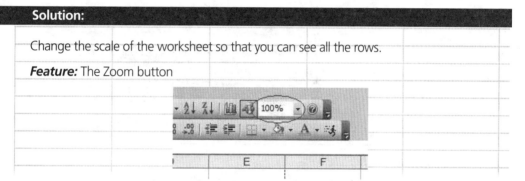

- Click the Zoom button and choose 75%. You can now see the entire page.

Hint:

You can type in any number from 10 to 400 to change the scale. The Zoom feature does not affect how the report prints.

- Now that you can see the entire area, apply the AutoFormat to the remaining sections. Make sure that you select the YTD Total rows in each section.

Now that you have all the AutoFormats in place, it's time to remove the decimal points from the numbers.

Change the decimals from two to none. When you select an entire column, any formatting you apply to the column will affect all the cells in the column.

Feature: The Decrease Decimal button

Step 1

- Select the column headers C, D, E and F

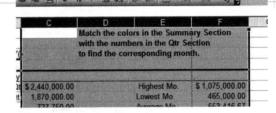

Step 2

- Click the Decrease Decimal button twice to remove the decimals

Hint:

If for some reason the decimals do not change, you'll have to select the individual number ranges to decrease the decimals.

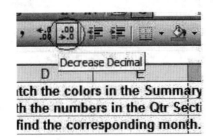

You have created all the formulas and applied all the formatting. You should be able to save the workbook and print the report. You want to review the report to make sure you've dotted all the i's and crossed all the t's. You take a quick look at Print Preview before you finalize the report.

- Click the Print Preview button

- The color coding to match the Summary Section to the Data Area has disappeared

- Repeat the color coding steps to match the Summary Section numbers with the Quarter Sections numbers

You also see that Column A is very wide and the Preview stops at the March numbers. Note the Next button to the far top right of the screen. It is active and indicates there is another page. The button next to it, "Previous," is not active. These buttons allow you to move from page to page.

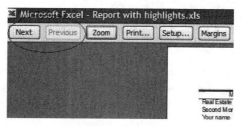

Click on it and you see that one column flows over to page two.

Close Print Preview and fix the problems.

Feature: Column/row tick lines

Step 1

Replace all the color coding to match the Summary Section to the Quarter/Month Sections as previously explained.

Step 2

Reduce the width of column A.

Tick lines are the lines that separate the column headers (A, B, C, etc.) and the row headers 1-2-3, etc. (Excel® has no specific term for these lines. Tick lines are the lines on a ruler indicating width.)

A1	▼	ƒₓ	My MortgageCompany		
	A		B	C	
1	My MortgageCompany				
2	Real Estate Loan Department				L
3	Second Mortgage Report 2007				M
4	Your name				w
5	As of		=TODAY()		tc

To make the column narrower:

- Hover the cross cursor over the tick line between columns A and B until it changes to a double-sided arrow

- Click and drag to the left until column A is an appropriate width

Hint:

You don't want to do this here, but if you double-click a tick line, Excel® automatically adjusts the width/height to fit the widest cell or row.

Step 3

You also notice that cell A1 doesn't show the entire company's name. It is center aligned and the cell is now too narrow to show the whole name. To change the alignment of cell A1:

- Click cell A1

- Click the Align Left button

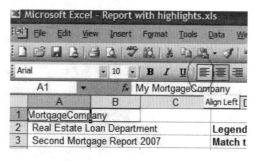

You have fixed the problems, and your report should be finished. A quick check of Print Preview verifies that it's all on one page and ready to print and distribute. You want to print 10 copies of the report. You'll deliver nine copies to your boss and keep one for your own records.

Before you print, save the worksheet.

Click the Save button on the Standard toolbar, or click File > Save As to name and save the worksheet.

Hint:

When you click the Save button, if the worksheet has not yet been saved, the Save As dialog box opens; if the worksheet has already been saved, the Save button saves the current worksheet with the same name.

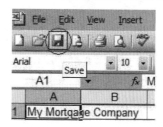

Solution:

Print the report.

Feature: The Print command

You can print from the Print Preview page by clicking on the Print button.

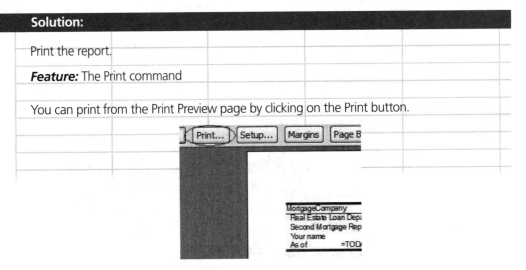

When you click the Print button, the Print dialog box opens.

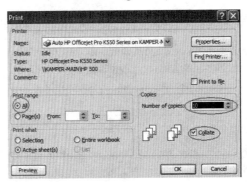

You don't want just one copy of the worksheet, you want 10 copies, so change the Number of Copies to 10. You also want the printer to collate the copies so you leave that box checked. (***Note:*** Printers vary widely. Some do not have the Collate feature.)

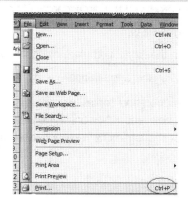

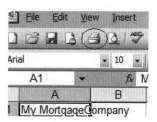

Compare your report to the workbook *Second Mortgage Report 2007.xls* on the accompanying CD.

Results

You now have completed the report and are quite pleased with it. It provides the required information:

- Quarter 3 produced the largest amount of loans
- Quarter 4, the least
- The month that produced the most loans was May; the least, January
- It is professional in appearance

You submit the report and copies to your boss, who reviews it and tells you that it is just the information he needed. Not only is he pleased with it, but after his meeting he lets you know that senior management was impressed with the report and wanted to know who created it.

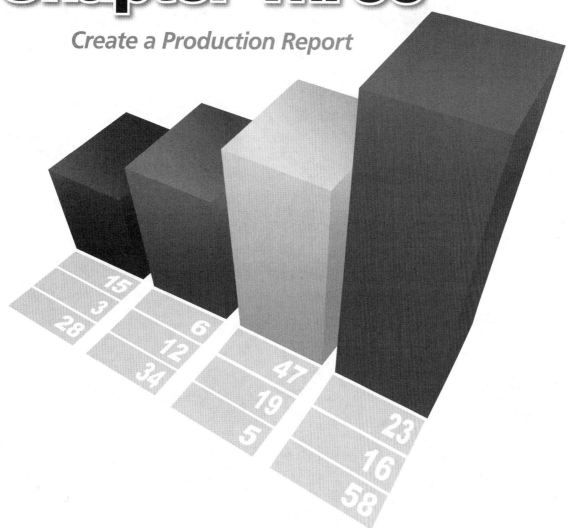

Chapter Three

Create a Production Report

What have your sales been?

The title of your position is Loan Representative. You work at a large mortgage company. Now that you have finished the special report (quite successfully), which recorded sales in the Second Mortgage Loan department, you can look after your own responsibilities. You decide it's time you tracked your own loan production.

Your primary responsibility is to solicit home mortgage loans from various sources including Realtors, direct contact with prospective borrowers, walk-ins when you have office responsibilities, and others. You've been quite successful, but haven't been keeping track of the loans you've been getting or information about those loans.

Solution:

Create a Production Report.

Remembering to keep the end in mind, you spend some time thinking about what kind of information you want to get from the report. This determines how you'll design the spreadsheet and what data to use to generate the information you want. You decide the data should at least include:

- Borrowers' names
- Type of loan—Conventional, FHA or VA
- Date closed (when the loan was actually funded)
- Loan amounts

Properly set up, this data should provide you with information such as:

- The total of all the loans you generated
- Loan production information broken down by month

You insert the title and experiment with the information and the way you'll design the report. (To follow along, open the workbook *Experiment.xls* on the accompanying CD.)

	A	B	C	D
1	My Mortgage Company			
2	Real Estate Loan Department			
3	Loan Production Report			
4	Your name			
5	Date:	=Today()		
6				
7				
8				
9				
10	Last Name	Type	Date Closed	Loan Amt
11	Smith	Conv	1/10/2008	100000
12	Smith	Conv	1/11/2008	150000
13	DeAngelo	Conv	1/22/2008	200000
14	Annkam	FHA	1/25/2008	75000
15	Burse	Conv	1/29/2008	126000

You have a good start on the report, but after further consideration, you see it doesn't contain all the information you want to track. After more thought you add more requirements to the minimal information you've already considered. This is the information you want:

- *The borrower's first name and last name.* You notice you have two borrowers with Smith as their last name. Because you track the loans by borrower, you must be able to distinguish one loan from another.

- *Loan type.* There are different loan limits and other requirements for the different types of loans. Usually the government-insured loans take longer to process and approve. You want to originate loans that are easy to process, approve and close. You would prefer more conventional loans than government loans.

- *Lead contact for the loan.* You want to report on the loan approval progress to your leads so you can provide good service and develop more loans; the faster the loan is approved and closed, the better.

- *Location of the properties.* You want to find out where you are generating the loans from. Some areas produce more loans than others, so you want to spend more time originating loans in those locations. You also want to find out if some areas of your territory produce larger loans than others.

- *Origination and closed dates.* This helps you track loan progress.

- *How long it takes to get your loans approved and closed*

- *Loan amounts*

- *Totals*

Modify the proposed Production Report to include all the information you want. You have to add more columns for the data: First Name, Lead, Location, Origination Date and Closing Date. You add a column to the left of the Type column for the First Name.

Feature: Insert columns or rows

Step 1

Add (insert) columns. The data area of the report begins in row 10. (If you've followed along, the workbook *Experiment.xls* from the accompanying CD is already open.)

You use the same procedure to insert columns and rows. Columns are inserted to the left of the active cell; rows are inserted above the active cell. You can use the same procedure to delete rows or columns. Instead of Insert, choose Delete from the menu after you right-click.

Add a column between columns A and B for the first name of the borrower:

- Hover the cursor over the column B header until a downward pointing arrow appears

- Right-click and choose Insert from the menu

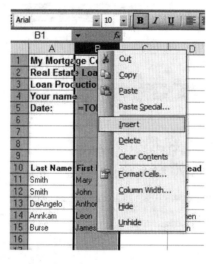

- A blank column is inserted to the left
- Click on cell B10 and type `First Name` in cell B10

Step 2

Add three columns to the left of column C to make room for the Lead, Location and Orig. Date headers:

- Select columns D, E and F
- Hover the cursor over a column header until it turns into a downward pointing arrow, as shown above
- Right-click and choose Insert from the menu

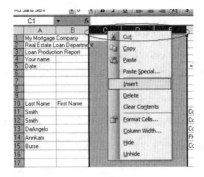

- Insert the headers Lead, Location and Orig. Date in cells C10, D10 and E10

Situation:

As long as you entered the title information, you may as well format it and the column headers.

Solution:

Bold cell contents and center the header cells.

Features: The Bold button and Align Center

- Select cells A1 though B5

- Press the CTRL key and click cell B5 and the row header 10

- Click the Bold button

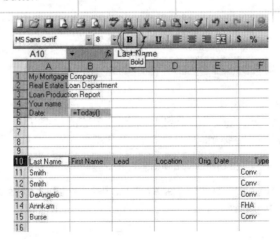

You want to center the header cells in row 10:

- Select row 10

- Click the Align Center button

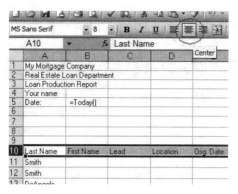

You finalize (for the time being) the design for your Production Report and input the data in the new columns. (Your report should now look like the file *Sales Report.xls* on the accompanying CD.)

	A	B	C	D	E	F	G	H
1	**My Mortgage Company**			Formula Bar				
9								
10	**Last Name**	**First Name**	**Type**	**Lead**	**Location**	**Orig. Date**	**Date Closed**	**Loan Amt**
11	Annkam	Leon	FHA	Ferchen	60129	11/23/2007	1/25/2008	75000
12	Burse	James	Conv	Burton	60101	12/6/2007	1/29/2008	126000
13	DeAngelo	Anthony	Conv	Jones	60116	12/20/2007	1/22/2008	200000
14	Smith	John	Conv	Baker	60108	11/29/2007	1/11/2008	150000
15	Smith	Mary	Conv	Jones	60101	12/3/2007	1/10/2008	100000
16	**Total**							
17								

Now that you have determined the design and inserted the rest of the loan data, you stop to think about how to best get the information out of the report.

You could simply use the spreadsheet as a normal spreadsheet, but that would require creating a number of different formulas and functions (which requires a lot of work).

Treat your spreadsheet as a list. A list is a series of data, either numbers or text—a range—that is surrounded by blank rows and blank columns. The spreadsheet you are creating qualifies as a list. (**Note:** The list option was added to Excel® 2003 and does not appear in earlier versions.)

A list has a number of useful features, some of which are:

- It has functions built into it, so you don't have to manually enter the functions to get the needed information

- You can easily sort the information by any column or columns

- You can filter the data to show only what you want to show. This is very useful when you intend to display or print only certain information and not the entire list.

- When you add Records, you automatically create new rows (in a list, the columns are called Fields; the rows are called Records)

If you wish to follow along with the steps to create the list, open the file *Sales Report.xls* from the accompanying CD. The steps are simple:

- Make sure that the data area has an empty row at the top and bottom of the data range and an empty column to the right and left of the data range (column A and row 1 qualify as an empty column or row)

- Click on any cell in the list

- Click Data > List > Create List

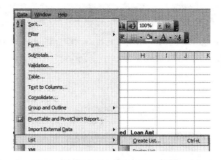

The Create List dialog box appears. It identifies the list range and that the list has Headers. The Headers are also called "fields."

- Click OK or press ENTER

A list adds a number of things to the data:

- The field names have sprouted list arrows (downward pointing arrows in boxes)

- All the cells in the list are selected

- A blue asterisk appears in cell A16, indicating you would begin adding data in the form of new records by clicking in that cell

- The list toolbar appears

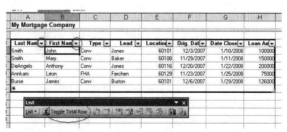

Hint:

Toolbars may float (as in the figure), be docked with the other toolbars at the top or docked to any side of the sheet. If yours doesn't readily appear, check the area at the top of the worksheet below the other toolbars.

You're now ready to get information from the list. Some of the first things you want to know are your loan production numbers:

- Total loan amount produced

- Largest, smallest and average loan amounts

- Number of loans you originated

Solution:

Use the built-in functions of a list to get the information without having to create them manually.

Feature: Toggle Total Row button on the List toolbar

Step 1

You want to know the total loan amount you produced. In the workbook *Sales Report.xls*:

- Click cell H16

- Click the Toggle Total Row button on the List toolbar

The Total row is added to the list and the Total Loan Amount you originated appears in cell H17.

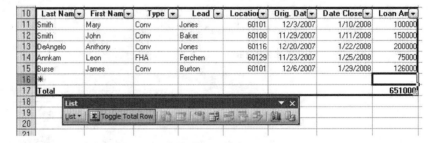

	Last Nam ▼	First Nam ▼	Type ▼	Lead ▼	Locatio ▼	Orig. Dat ▼	Date Close ▼	Loan Am ▼
11	Smith	Mary	Conv	Jones	60101	12/3/2007	1/10/2008	100000
12	Smith	John	Conv	Baker	60108	11/29/2007	1/11/2008	150000
13	DeAngelo	Anthony	Conv	Jones	60116	12/20/2007	1/22/2008	200000
14	Annkam	Leon	FHA	Ferchen	60129	11/23/2007	1/25/2008	75000
15	Burse	James	Conv	Burton	60101	12/6/2007	1/29/2008	126000
16	*							
17	Total							651000

Hint:

Because the cell with the blue asterisk is above the Total row, the Total row is always at the bottom of the list. When you add records, the Total row is always the last row.

Step 2

You also want to know the MAX, MIN and AVERAGE loan amounts and the number of loans you originated:

- Click on cell H17, the Total Loan Amount, and it sprouts a list arrow to the right

- Click the list arrow and choose the function you want from the nine listed

Situation:

You notice that the ZIP Codes are aligned to the right of the cells. They have been input as numbers, but they are actually text. You don't want to accidentally total that column.

Solution:

Format the Location column as text.

Features: Format cells as text and select entire columns/rows

Step 1

- If you entered the Count function in cell E17, change it to "None," the first item on the list (see the previous figure)

- Click in a blank cell

- Right-click on the column header E to select the entire column
- Choose Format Cells from the list

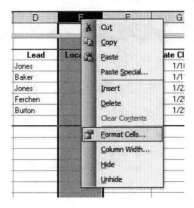

Step 2

From the dialog box that appears:

- Make sure the Number tab is selected
- Click Text > OK

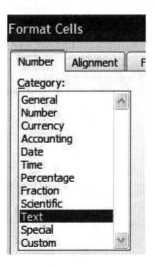

The ZIP Codes now align as text, to the left of the cells.

You'd like to see the loans listed by last name so you can track them better.

Sort the loans by last name.

Features: Sort buttons

To sort the data by last names:

- Click in any cell in the Last Name field, as shown below

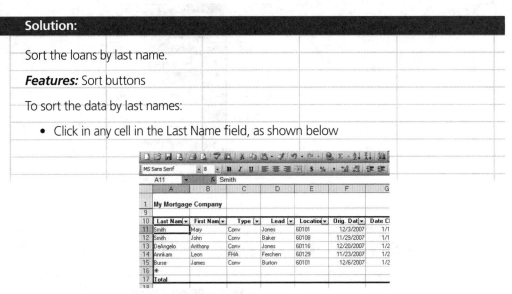

- Click on the Sort A – Z button (or the Z – A button to reverse the sort) on the Standard toolbar

You've sorted the loans by last name.

You notice there are two borrowers with the last name "Smith." You want to sort the borrowers first by last name, then by first name.

Sort by last name, then first name.

Features: Data > Sort

- Click on any cell in the list
- Click Data > Sort. The Sort dialog box appears.

- Click the "Sort by" box list arrow and change it to Last Name
- Click the list arrow in the "Then by" box and change it to First Name
- Notice that the Ascending radio buttons are active
- Click OK

You've sorted the columns properly by last name, then by first name—John Smith, then Mary Smith.

Hint:

When sorting do not select individual cells and then use the Sort command. If you do that you sort only the data in the selected cells, not all the data in the list.

In addition to the loan production amounts, you also want to find out where in your territory you are generating loans. You also want to know if the loan amounts are smaller in one location than another.

Filter the locations to show loans originated only in specific ZIP Codes. A great feature of a list is that you can filter the information, that is, filter out the data you don't want to see. This is done by using the list arrows to the right of the field names and selecting the information you want to appear.

Feature: Filter arrows

You want to know which of your loans are on properties located only in ZIP Code 60101:

- Click on the list arrow to the right of the Location field

- Choose 60101

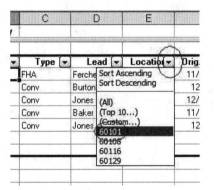

You have loans on two properties located in ZIP Code 60101 which amount to a total of $226,000. (Notice that rows 11, 13 and 14 have been filtered out.)

	Last Name ⏷	First Name ⏷	Type ⏷	Lead ⏷	Location ⏷	Orig.Date ⏷	Date Close ⏷	Loan Amt ⏷
12	Burse	James	Conv	Burton	60101	12/6/2007	1/29/2008	126000
15	Smith	Mary	Conv	Jones	60101	12/3/2007	1/10/2008	100000
16	*							
17	Total							226000

To remove the filter:

- Click back on the Location list arrow (which has now turned blue)
- Click on All

Situation:

You want to find out which loans are located in ZIP Codes 60101 and 60108.

Solution:

Filter for ZIP Codes 60101 and 60108.

Feature: The Custom filter

- Click in any cell in the Location column
- Click the list arrow in the header
- Choose Custom from the list

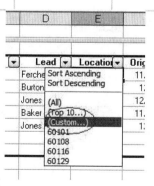

The Custom AutoFilter dialog box appears.

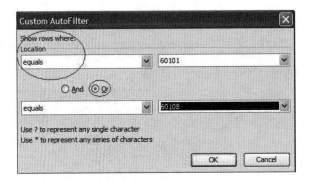

- In the Location area, select equals from the list arrow

- Choose 60101 in the box to the right

- Choose the Or radio button

- Choose "equals" and "60108" as indicated in the figure above

- Click OK

Only the data in those locations shows.

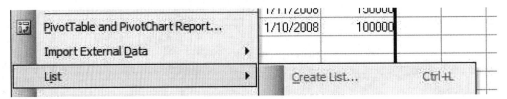

You want to be able to evaluate your leads. For example, which Realtors are providing the most loans, and/or what type of loan?

Filter the data using the Lead field following the steps outlined previously.

- If you filtered the loans by location, click back on the Location list arrow and change it to All

- Use the filter list arrow in the Lead field to filter the loans by individual lead (you find that Jones is providing you with the most leads)

- Experiment with the other filter buttons to see how you can use them to find more details about the loans

- Now that you have analyzed the data, you want to remove the list

- Click Data > List > Convert to Range

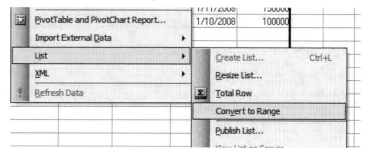

Results

As a result of the information contained in your Production Report, you determine that:

- The loans you are getting are all small loan amounts. (The current maximum loan amount for conventional and VA loans is $417,000; the current maximum FHA loan amount is $200,150. These maximums are subject to change.)

- The Realtors you have been cultivating for leads have been giving you only smaller loans. You'll have to get them to refer larger loans.

- You have to develop new leads

- You've been limiting yourself to areas that have produced only lower loan amounts. You need to broaden your production area.

- You implement what your list tells you:

  — You discuss with your present leads the size of the loans you are getting. As a result of the information from your Production Report, you are giving better service, and they refer larger loans to you.

  — You expand your production area

  — You develop new leads

As a result, your loan production has greatly improved. You have made good use of the data.

Last Name	First Name	Type	Lead	Location	Orig. Date	Date Closed	Loan Amt
Smith	Mary	Conv	Baker	60108	11/29/2007	1/11/2008	150000
Burse	James	Conv	Burton	60101	12/6/2007	1/29/2008	126000
Annkam	Leon	FHA	Ferchen	60129	11/23/2007	1/25/2008	75000
Smith	John	Conv	Jones	60101	12/3/2007	1/10/2008	100000
DeAngelo	Anthony	Conv	Jones	60116	12/20/2007	1/22/2008	200000
Rodgers	Wolfgang	Conv	Jones	60119	1/10/2008	3/3/2008	356000
Taber	David	Conv	Northam	60101	2/15/2008	3/31/2008	315000
Prewitt	Gene	FHA	Sender	60129	1/22/2008	3/17/2008	175000
Fernandez	Jose	VA	Sender	60118	2/1/2008	3/13/2008	364200
Abelt	William	Conv	Seymour	60128	2/6/2008	3/19/2008	295150
*							
Total							2156350

Chapter Four

Create a Commission Report

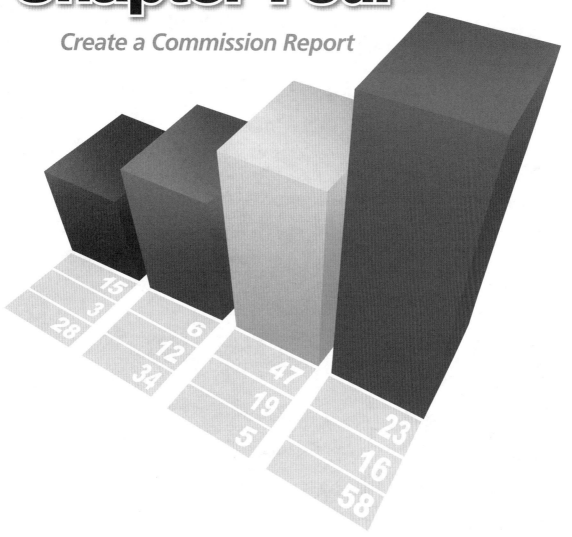

How much would your commission be if ... ?

Your boss has a new request for you. Senior management is considering different salary arrangements for the Second Mortgage Loan department. He mentions that since you did such a good job on the previous report, they have specifically requested that you prepare the new one. They would like the report ASAP. The report title is to be: "Tentative Commission Report." Also, the report is to be very confidential. They don't want it to be a subject for water cooler discussion.

Rather than straight salary, management is considering a payroll arrangement for the sales reps that is part salary and part commission. The theory is that the reps will produce more loans if paid partially by commission because of the potential for increased income.

You already have the second mortgage loan production data for last year. Management would like to know:

- How much commission would have been paid to the sales reps last year had they been using the proposed arrangement (they want to compare last year's actual salaries to what the total salaries would have been if the sales reps were paid on the salary plus commission basis)

- What percent each sales rep contributed to total production, and if any rep's production fell below the proposed quota

The proposed commission schedule is as follows:

- Commission would be paid at the end of every quarter, based on quarterly sales

- The sales quota is $500,000 for the quarter

- If sales reach the quota or exceed it, the commission rate is .25%

- If sales are below quota, the commission rate is .125%

Design and create a Commission Report.

After some consideration and experimentation, you decide on the following design for your report.

	A	B	C	D	E	F	G	H	I	J	K	L
1	CONFIDENTIAL											
2	My Mortgage Company											
10		Qtr 1 Totals			Qtr 2 Totals		Qtr 3 Totals				Qtr 4Totals	
11	Name	Sales	% of Total	Comm. Ar	Sales	%of Total	Sales	%of Total	Comm. Ar	Sales	%of Total	Comr
12	Larry											
13	Moe											
14	Curley											
15	Total Sales											
16												
17												

In its present stage, the information flows all the way out to column P, which requires at least two pages. This will require some design changes for printing purposes, but it is the best design to use for the report.

The time factor also requires that you prepare the report as quickly as possible. You enter the title information and a legend that indicates the quota amount, the commission rates and the indication of whether the quota has not been met. (If you want to follow along, open the file *Commission Report Layout.xls* from the accompanying CD.)

Features: Font size, Text Box, activating a toolbar, the Drawing toolbar, size, move and format a text box and format borders

Step 1

Type the title information. Because the report will print out on two pages, you want the sales reps' names to appear on the second page, but not the title information. You enter the title information in column B, starting in cell B1; the sales reps' names in column A, starting in cell A11.

- Click on cell B1. You want to alert the readers about the confidentiality of the report.
- Press the CAPS LOCK key and type the word CONFIDENTIAL
- Press the green checkmark on the Formula bar to keep from moving the active cell
- Still in cell B1, click the Font Size tool on the Standard toolbar
- Change the font size to 12 points

<u>Hint:</u>

There are 72 points in one inch.

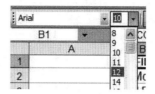

- In cells B2 through B8, enter the following text:

    — My Mortgage Company

    — Real Estate Loan Department

    — Tentative Report

    — Second Mortgage Department

    — Loan information based on 2007 sales figures

    — Date:

    — Prepared by: Your Name

- In cell C7 enter the formula =Today() to always bring up the current date when the worksheet is opened

Step 2

Create the Legend area and type in the quota data. You will create a text box to hold the Legend information.

- Make sure the Drawing toolbar is open. It is usually docked at the bottom of the spreadsheet.

Hint:

If you don't see the Drawing toolbar, right-click on any toolbar. If the Drawing toolbar has a check in front of it, it is already open. If there is no checkmark, click to open it.

- Click the Text Box button on the Drawing toolbar

Your cursor shape changes to a small upside down black T ($\perp$) that allows you to draw the text box.

- Click and drag to draw the text box in cell F1

- Type the quota data:

  - If sales meet or exceed $500,000 per quarter, the commission amount is .25%

  - If less than $500,000, .125%

  - If the quota is not met, the cell has a red background

- Size the text box appropriately by clicking on one of the handles and place it appropriately

Hint:

To size a text box, a graphic or a chart, hover the cursor over one of the sizing handles until it turns into a double arrow. (Refer to the Cursor Shapes Table in the Introduction.) Click and drag to size the text box appropriately.

If sales meet or exceed $500,000 per quarter, the commission amount is .25%;
If less than $500,000, .125%.
If the quota is not met, the cell has a red background.

Step 3

Move the box to the appropriate location.

- Hover the cursor over the border of the text box until it changes to a 4-headed arrow

- Click and drag to the appropriate location

Hint:

To move a text box, a graphic or a chart, hover the cursor over a shaded border until it changes to a 4-headed arrow. (Refer to the Cursor Shapes Table in the Introduction.) Click and drag to the appropriate location.

Step 4

Change the size and color of the lines around the text box to make it stand out.

- Hover the cursor over a shaded border of the text box until it changes into a 4-headed arrow

- Right-click

- Choose Format Text Box …

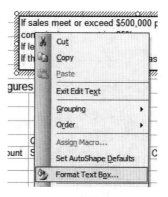

In the dialog box that opens:

- Click the Colors and Lines tab

- Change the line color to violet (to match the company's colors)

- Change the weight to 1.5 points

- Click OK

- Click away from the text box

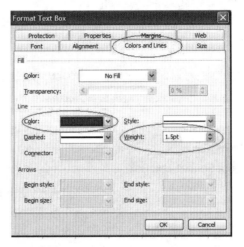

Your workbook should look similar to *Commission Report layout 2.xls* on the accompanying CD.

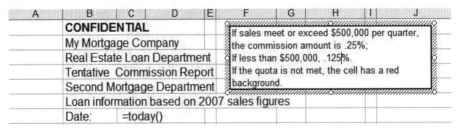

You have inserted the title data and quota information and finalized the design. You already have the sales data for Larry, Moe and Curley in the workbook Second Mortgage Report 2007. You want to use that data in this report, but don't want to re-type it. Simply copying the information won't do the job for you because you want the data to be updated if there is any change in the data.

Solution:

Link the cells. A link is simply an equation in one cell (the Dependent cell) that duplicates the data in the original cell (the Source cell). You have already used a link when you clicked on a cell when creating a formula.

Linking cells is a simple, speedy, efficient and accurate way to duplicate and update information from one place to another. Updating is an especially good feature. If the information in the Source cell changes, the Dependent cell changes as well.

Feature: Links

The steps to create a link are simple:

Step 1

- Click on the cell you want to copy the information to—the Dependent cell

- Type =

Step 2

- Click on the cell you want to link—the Source cell

- Press ENTER

- You can link cells to:

    — Another cell in the same worksheet

    — A cell in another worksheet in the same workbook

    — A cell in a different workbook

    — A file in a different program, such as Microsoft® Word. You can link copied cells or an object, such as a chart, to another program using the Paste Special command.

- Linked cells are updated automatically:
  — For changes made within the same worksheet and/or on a different worksheet within the same workbook
  — For changes made in a different workbook/file, if both the Source and Dependent workbook/file are open, the information is updated automatically
  — If the Dependent workbook/file is open and the Source workbook/file is not, the Dependent cells are updated when the appropriate workbook opens
  — If the Source workbook/file is not open, you receive a prompt that asks if you want to update the links

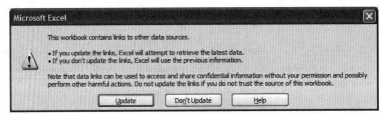

Situation:

You want to link the sales totals from *Second Mortgage Report 2007.xls* (the Source workbook) to the sales totals in *Commission Report layout2.xls* (the Dependent workbook).

Solution:

It is easier to link the cells from one worksheet to the other if you can see them both at the same time.

Features: Compare worksheets side by side, rearrange worksheets

You want to view both worksheets at the same time. (If you want to follow along, open the workbook *Commission Report layout 2.xls* if you haven't done so already, and the *Second Mortgage Report 2007.xls* workbook.)

Step 1

- Make sure that only these two workbooks are open

- Click Window to see the menu selections

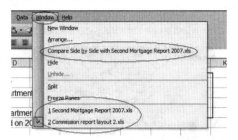

There are a number of options under the Window menu:

- New Window opens another copy of the active worksheet with the extension "*.xls:2*"

- Arrange provides you with the choices for how you want to see the currently open worksheets

- Compare Side by Side displays open worksheets side by side

- The Split and Freeze Panes options allow you to display different parts of the same worksheet at the same time. As you scroll down or sideways, you always have the rows/columns to the right of, or above, the split visible.

Step 2

- Choose Compare Side by Side so you can see both workbooks at the same time next to each other (you may have to size the windows to see as much of them as you can at any given time)

You now can see both worksheets side by side.

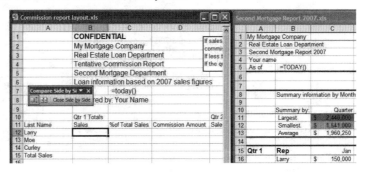

Hint:

You can manually resize an open worksheet(s). Click the Restore Window button in Excel®. It acts on the open worksheet and resizes it. If more than one worksheet is open, it resizes all of them.

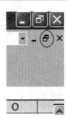

Hover the cursor over any side or corner border. The cursor changes to a double-sided "sizing" arrow. (Refer to the Cursor Shapes Table in the Introduction.)

- Click and drag on any side border—top, bottom, left or right—to size the item horizontally or vertically. This may distort the image. If you click and drag on a corner arrow to size the image, it sizes it proportionally, without distortion.

- Microsoft® provides the same procedure to show two or more open programs at the same time, such as Word and Excel®. Use the Restore Down button in the Title bar.

- **Note:** You can split two or more programs automatically. With two programs open full size, not minimized:
    - Right-click an empty area on the Windows taskbar (sometimes hidden at the bottom of the screen) and choose Tile Windows Horizontally or Tile Windows Vertically

Step 3

Notice the Compare Side by Side toolbar that opened.

The first button on the left is the Synchronous Scrolling button which is active by default. If you scroll in one window, the other window scrolls along with it. Click that button to turn the feature off. (The second button from the left changes the arrangement from vertical to horizontal.) Since you won't need this toolbar further, Click the X in the Title bar to turn it off.

Step 4

Now that you can see both worksheets, link the appropriate cells.

- Click anywhere on the Commission Report Layout 2 worksheet to activate it
- Click on cell B12, the Dependent cell

Hint:

You have to click twice. One click activates the worksheet, the second click activates the cell.

- Type =

- Click anywhere on the Second Mortgage Report 2007 worksheet to activate it

- Click on cell F16, the Source cell (you may have to scroll to see it)

- Press ENTER

The cells are linked. Note the cell reference in the Formula bar for cell B12 in the *Commission Report layout 2.xls* worksheet.

f_x ='[Second Mortgage Report 2007.xls]Sheet1'!$F$16

It contains:

- The name of the source workbook: "Second Mortgage Report 2007"

- The worksheet in the workbook "Sheet 1!"

- The cell reference "$F$16"

Hint:

The dollar signs ($) indicate absolute referencing. If you copy the formula, the reference to cell F16 will not change; without the dollar signs, relative referencing would change the cell reference.

Use the same (somewhat tedious) technique to:

- Link cells B13, 14 and 15 in Commission Report Layout 2 to cells F17, 18 and 19 in Second Mortgage Report 2007

Hint:

Remember that you have to click first on the worksheet to activate it and a second time to click on the cell.

- Link cells E12, 13, 14 and 15 in the Dependent worksheet to cells F24, 25, 26 and 27 in the Source worksheet

Hint:

You might see a series of # symbols in a cell, such as: "#######." That indicates that the cell is too narrow to see the entire number. Make the column wider to show the entire amount.

- Link cells G12, 13, 14 and 15 to cells F32, 33, 34 and 35

- Link cells J12, 13, 14 and 15 to cells J40, 41, 42 and 43

You have the quarterly sales numbers for each sales rep. You want to show the sales reps' loans for the entire year in cells M12 through M15.

Create the formulas.

- Create the formula for cell M12 using techniques previously explained. When finished it should read: "=B12+E12+G12+J12."

- Copy the formula down to the appropriate cells

- Your worksheet should look like *Commission Report layout 3.xls* on the accompanying CD. You have successfully linked the required cells.

Since you no longer need the Second Mortgage Report 2007 workbook, close it and maximize the remaining worksheet.

Now that you have the sales data and the totals, the next step is to determine which rep is producing the largest percent of loans.

Create the formulas for % of Sales. Divide each sales rep's sales by the total amount of sales; for example, Larry's Quarter 1 sales ($475,000) divided by the Quarter 1 Total sales ($1,870,000) returns.

Feature: Absolute referencing

Step 1

- Click on cell C12 in the Commission Report Layout 3 worksheet

- Press =

- Click on cell B12 to get Larry's sales amount for Quarter 1

- Press the / key to divide

- Click on cell B15 to get the total sales for all the reps in Quarter 1, but don't press ENTER yet! You want to use Absolute Referencing to copy the formula.

- Press the F4 function key at the top of your keyboard before you press ENTER. This inserts a dollar sign in front of the row reference and another in front of the column reference. This keep this cell reference "absolute"—unchanging—when you copy it to other cells.

- Click the green checkmark on the Formula bar, rather than pressing ENTER, so you don't have to reposition the active cell. This enters the formula in cell C12 and keeps it the active cell. The formula reads: "=B12/$B$15."

Step 2

- Copy the formula down to cells C13, 14 and 15 using the AutoFill tool. For example, the formula in cell C13 should read: "=B13/$B$15," etc.

Situation:

The numbers are in decimals, not percentages.

Solution:

Change the number formatting from decimals to percentages.

Feature: The Percent Style button

While cells C12 through C15 are still selected:

- Click the Percent Style button on the Formatting toolbar to show the numbers as percents

Step 3

Create the formulas and copy them with the appropriate cell references for each sales rep in Quarters 2, 3 and 4 and for the YTD percentages, as above:

- The formula in cell F12 should read "=E12/$E$15"
- The formula in cell I12 should read "=H12/$H$15"
- The formula in cell L12 should read "=K12/$K$15"
- The formula in cell N12 should read "=M12/$M$15"

Hint:

Make sure that the results all show as percents and not decimals.

Situation:

Now that you have the Percent of Sales numbers, you want to create the formulas for the Commission Amount for each sales rep. To do this, you have to determine whether the sales reps made their quotas or not. If sales are below the quota of $500,000 per quarter, the commission rate is .125%; if sales are equal to or more than the quota, the commission rate is .25%.

Solution:

Create the formulas for the commission amounts.

Feature: The IF function. The IF function makes logical decisions. Its logic is as follows: "If something is true, do this; if it's not true, do that."

In cell D12, for example, Larry's Commission Amount, the function would be interpreted to read: "If the amount in cell B12 (Larry's sales) is greater than or equal to $500,000, multiply cell B12 (Larry's sales) by .25%; if it's less than $500,000, multiply cell B12 (Larry's sales) by .125%."

The IF function is easy to put together if you use the Function Wizard.

Step 1

- Click on cell D12, where you want Larry's commission

- Click the *fx* button on the Formula bar

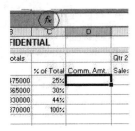

Step 2

- In the Insert Function dialog box that opens, choose Logical from the "Or select a category" box (it might also be in the Most Recently Used category)

- From the list, choose IF

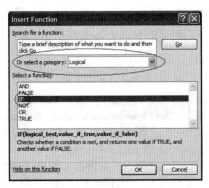

- Click OK and the Function Arguments dialog box appears

- The cursor is located in the Logical_test box

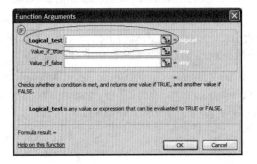

Step 3

- Click cell B12—the cell that contains Larry's sales for Quarter 1

- Type > =500000 (so far the function reads: "If cell B12 is greater than or equal to 500,000 …")

- Press the TAB key to move the cursor to the Value_if_true box

- Click cell B12

- Type *.25% (So far the function reads "If cell B12 is greater than or equal to 500,000, multiply cell B12 by 0.25%")

- Press the TAB key to move the cursor to the Value_if_false box

- Click cell B12

- Type *.125% (the function reads, "If cell B12 is greater than or equal to 500,000, multiply cell B12 by .25%" or, "If cell B12 is less than 500,000, multiply cell B12 by 0.125%")

- Click OK

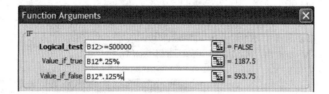

Larry's commission for Quarter 1 is $593.75.The final formula is: "=IF(B12>=500000,B12 *0.25%,B12*0.125%)."

Hint:

To the right of each box are words/numbers that indicate the status of the function. You note that if Larry had produced more than $500,000 in loans, his commission would have been $1,187.50.

Step 4

- Make sure you're still in cell D12

- Copy the function down using the AutoFill tool

- While the cells are still selected, format them as dollars. Click on the $ (the Currency Style button on the Formatting toolbar).

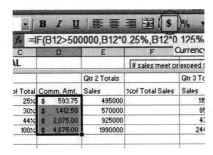

Hint:

The Currency Style button actually applies the Accounting style, not the Currency style. (You can check the differences by clicking Format > Cells > the Number tab.) The Accounting style aligns dollar signs and decimal points for numbers with varying amounts of digits, e.g., $50.12 versus $5,000.00. The Currency style simply puts a dollar sign in front of the numbers without aligning them.

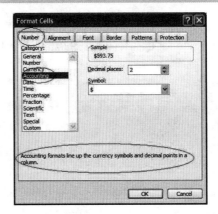

You have the commission amounts (formatted) for the sales reps for Quarter 1. You need the same information for the other quarters.

Create formulas for the commission amounts for the remaining Quarters and Total Commissions Paid. Because the layout of the columns for each quarter is the same, you can easily copy both the functions and formatting to the appropriate cells.

Create the formulas for the quarters. While cells D12 through D15 are still selected:

- Press CTRL + C (to copy the formulas)

- Click cell G12

- Press CTRL + V to paste the formulas (because of Relative Referencing, the formulas are correctly reproduced)

- Follow the same procedure to create the formulas for the Commission Amounts in the remaining quarters

Hint:

Because Excel® allows only one Paste command for each Copy/Cut command, you have to Press CTRL + C each time before you Paste.

You now have the Commission Amounts for each rep properly formatted for each quarter. You now need the formula for Total Commissions Paid:

- Click cell P12

- Create the formula for the Total Commissions Paid as usual and copy it down to the appropriate cells. The formula in cell P12 is "=D12+G12+J12+M12."

- If you followed along, your worksheet should look like *Commission report layout 4.xls* on the accompanying CD

Management's specific request was to indicate the sales reps whose sales fell below the quota.

If sales are less than the quota, you want to highlight the Total Sales cells with a color to call attention to them. You decide to apply a red background to any quarterly sales amount below $500,000.

Feature: Conditional Formatting

Conditional Formatting is similar to but easier to use than an IF statement. The conditional statement would simply be "If sales are less than $500,000 make the background of that cell a red color."

Step 1

- Select cells B12 through B14, the sales for Quarter 1 (do not include the total, cell B15)

Step 2

- Click Format > Conditional Formatting

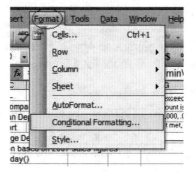

The Conditional Formatting dialog box opens. You want Condition 1 to be: "If the Cell Value is less than 500,000."

The default for Condition 1 is "between."

- Click the list arrow to the right of "between" and choose "less than" from the list

- Press Tab to move to the next box and type 500000

Step 3

- Click the Format button which opens the Format Cells dialog box

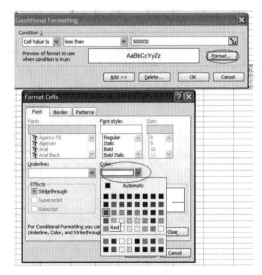

Step 4

- Click on the list arrow to the right of Color and choose a red color

- Click OK to return to the Conditional Format dialog box

- Click OK

Larry's sales for Quarter 1 fell below the quota; the others' did not.

Hint:

You can have more than one condition. For example, you could add a condition to turn cells green if sales are more than $750,000.

Situation:

You can paste the formatting with the Format Painter tool, but your worksheet is so wide you can't see all the columns. It would be easier to paste the formatting if you could see all the columns.

Solution:

Reduce the magnification.

Feature: The Zoom button

Step 1

- Click the Zoom tool on the Standard toolbar

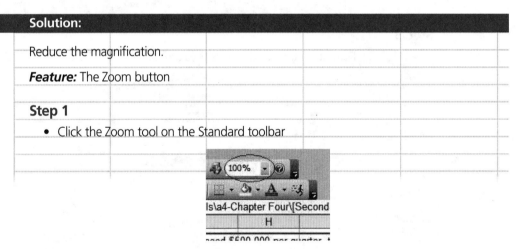

Step 2

- Type 70. This view allows you to easily see the cells you want to copy the formatting to.

Hint:

Changing the magnification on the screen does not change the font sizes. The worksheet prints at 100% whatever the zoom percent.

Step 3

- Click cell B12

- Double-click the Format Painter button and copy the formatting to cells E12 through E14; H12 through H14; and K12 to K14

- Click the Format Painter to turn it off

Hint:

Do not apply this formatting to the Total row.

If you followed along, your worksheet should now look like *Commission Report layout 5.xls* on the accompanying CD.

Situation:

The report meets the requests of management. You have the commissions, the percent each sales rep contributed to loan production and the indication of whose sales were below quota. Because this report is going to senior management, you want the report to look more professional. It needs better formatting.

One of the first things you notice in Print Preview is that the data for the quarters runs together and it's hard to see where one quarter stops and the other quarter begins.

Solution:

You would like more space between the quarters to better set them apart. To make the quarter information stand out better you insert columns between the quarters. (Columns are inserted to the left of the active cell; rows are inserted above.)

Feature: Insert columns (or rows)

Step 1

Insert a column between columns D and E

- Right-click the column E header

- Choose Insert from the list

Step 2

Insert columns between the remaining quarters and year end:

- Click—not right-click—on Column Header I

- Press Ctrl + Y to redo the Insert Column command

- Do the same for the columns between Quarter 4 Sales and Year End Totals. You should now have the following empty columns: E, I, M and Q.

Situation:

You intend to make these columns "spacer columns," so you want them to be fairly narrow. As mentioned earlier, you can size a column by clicking and dragging on the tick mark on the left side of the column head. Because you want all the spacer columns to be the same width, you choose not to use this method. You want to make each spacer column 1.5 characters wide.

Solution:

Size the spacer columns so they are all the same width.

Feature: Size columns

Step 1

- Right-click Column Header E

- Choose Column Width

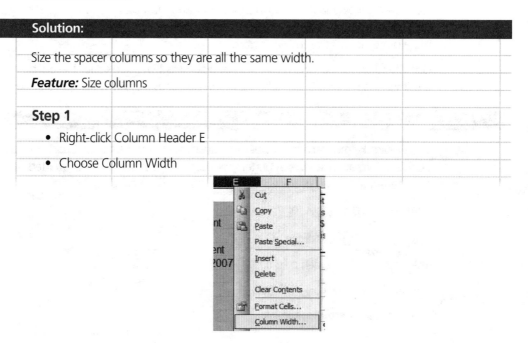

- Type 1.5 in the Column Width box
- Click OK

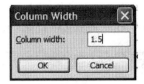

Step 2

Make the inserted columns the same width as Column E using the CTRL + Y method as above.

Situation:

The report is almost finished. You've spent a lot of time and energy to get to this point. You have the information but it is hard to read. There is only minimal formatting. To make the report more professional looking, you have to do more formatting. From experience you know that the AutoFormat tool changes the columns widths, alignment of cells and the height of columns, which you do not want to do. AutoFormat will not do the job for you here.

Solution:

Format the worksheet segment by segment.

The width of the text in some of the headers is not proportionate to the width of the numbers in the cells. For example, the "% of Total Sales" headers all contain sixteen digits including the space, while its widest content is only 4 digits, "100%."

Wrap the text in the column headers that are too wide and adjust their column widths.

Features: Cell Alignment and wrap text

Step 1

- Click on cell C11, "% of Total Sales"

- Click Format > Cells > the Alignment tab

- Click the Wrap Text box

- Click OK

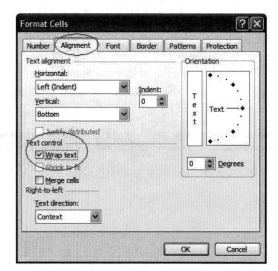

- Check the row height. It may now be too narrow to show the entire text.

9				
10		Qtr 1 Totals		
11	Name	Sales	% of Total	C
12	Larry	475000	25%	$
13	Moe	565000	30%	$
14	Curley	830000	44%	$
15	Total Sales	1870000	100%	$
16				

- Double-click the tick line between rows 11 and 12 to adjust the row height, if needed

10		Qtr 1 Totals			
				% of Total Sales	
11	Name	Sales		Sales	Cor
12	Larry		475000	25%	$
13	Moe		565000	30%	$
14	Curley		830000	44%	$
15	Total Sales		1870000	100%	$

Step 2

Center align the column:

- Click Column Header C
- Click the Align Center button

B	C	D	E
CONFIDENTIAL			
Qtr 1 Totals			Qtr 2
	% of Total		
Sales	Sales	Comm. Amt.	Sales
475000	25%	$ 593.75	
565000	30%	$ 1,412.50	
830000	44%	$ 2,075.00	
1870000	100%	$ 4,675.00	1

Step 3

Copy this formatting to the remaining "% of Total Sales" headers and appropriate cells:

- Double-click the Format Painter button
- Click on the column headers G, K, O and S
- Turn off the Format Painter
- Check the headers to make sure they are all the same (you may have to adjust some of the column widths)

Hint:

You can manually wrap text as you type by pressing the ALT key + ENTER where you want the text to break.

The column headers for "Comm. Amt." are still too wide for the rest of the column, but not by much.

Rotate the text.

Feature: Rotate text

Step 1

- Make sure you're in cell D11

- Click Format > Cells > Alignment

- In the Orientation box, click, drag and rotate the red diamond up to 45°

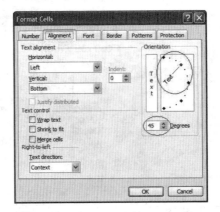

Step 2

- Use the Format Painter to format cells H11, L11 and P11 appropriately

The headers now take up less space.

- Copy this formatting to the other "Comm. Amt." headers

Situation:

Rows 10 and 11, the rows that contain the headers, would look better if they were centered and in bold text.

Solution:

Bold and Center the rows.

Step 1

- Select rows 10 and 11
- Click the Bold and Align Center buttons

Step 2

Standard accounting format indicates that the first number in a column of numbers and totals should have a dollar sign. Format the dollars in rows 12 and 15:

- Use the CTRL key to select all the cells in row 12 that have Larry's Sales numbers—cells B12, F12, J12 and N12; and all the cells in row 15 that have Total Sales—Cell B15, F15, J15 and N15

- Click the Currency Style button on the Formatting toolbar

- Decrease the decimals by two

Step 3

Standard accounting format indicates that dollars shown within a column should only have comma delimiters, no dollar signs.

- Use the CTRL key to select cells B13 and B14, D13 and 14, F13 and 14, H13 and 14, J13 and 14, L13 and 14, N13 and 14, P13 and 14, R13 and 14 and T13 and 14

- Click the Comma Style button on the Formatting toolbar

- Decrease the decimals by two

Step 4

Standard accounting format indicates that numbers followed by a total should have a single underline. Underline the cells in row 14 that indicate a total as follows:

- Click cell B12

- Press the SHIFT key and click on cell T14

- Use the Borders tool to single underline the numbers and percentages in row 14

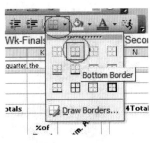

Step 5

Standard accounting format indicates that totals should have a double underline.

- Click cell B15

- Press the S<small>HIFT</small> key and click on cell T15

- Use the Borders tool on the Formatting toolbar to double underline the numbers and percentages in row 15

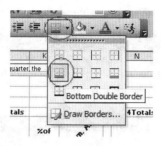

Situation:

To better delineate the quarters for a better appearance, the headers Qtr 1 Totals, Qtr 2 Totals, etc. should be centered over the cells.

Solution:

Center the quarter headers over the quarters' data.

Feature: Merge and Center

Step 1
- Select cells B10 through D10

Step 2
- Click the Merge and Center button

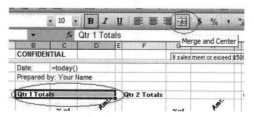

The header is centered over the appropriate columns.

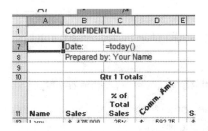

	A	B	C	D	E
1		CONFIDENTIAL			
7		Date:	=today()		
8		Prepared by: Your Name			
9					
10		Qtr 1 Totals			
11	Name	Sales	% of Total Sales	Comm. Amt.	S.
12	I	$ 475 000	25%	$ 593 75	$

- Repeat the process for the remaining quarters and the year end information

Situation:

You want to indicate that the report is confidential and insert page numbers at the bottom of each page.

Solution:

Add a footer to indicate that the workbook is confidential and insert page numbers.

Feature: Header and Footer

Hint:

You can access the Header and Footer dialog box by clicking on View > Header and Footer, by clicking on Page Setup in Print Preview, or by clicking on File > Page Setup. Use the latter—File > Page Setup because it activates all the tools in Page Setup. If you use the other avenues, the "Print titles" functions are inactive.

Step 1

- Click on File > Page Setup

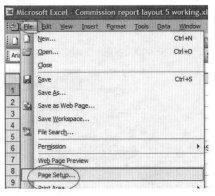

Step 2

In the Page Setup dialog box that appears:

- Click the Header/Footer tab

- Click the Custom Footer button

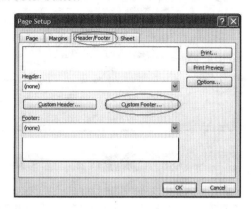

Step 3

- Click in the "Left section" area in the Footer dialog box

- Type CONFIDENTIAL

- Click in the "Center section" area

- Type Tentative Commission Report

- Click in the "Right section" area. You want the page numbers to read "Page x of x pages"

- Type Page and press the SPACE bar

- Click the # button to insert the page number and press the SPACE bar

- Type of and press the SPACE bar

- Click the ++ button to insert the total number of pages
- Click OK twice to return to the worksheet

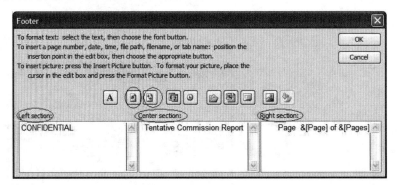

You check Print Preview to view the Footer. The Footer is fine, but you see that the report flows over to three pages. You want the spreadsheet to fit on two pages.

Solution:

Change the Page Orientation from Portrait to Landscape.

Step 1

- Click the Setup button while still in Print Preview

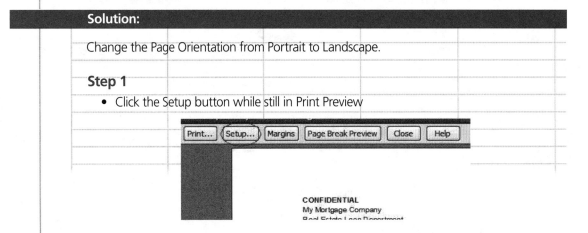

- Select the Page tab
- Click the Landscape radio button

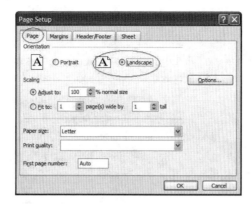

- Click OK and you return to Print Preview

Situation:

Print Preview shows that the worksheet now fits on two pages. You click the Next button and see that the second page doesn't include the reps' names, making it harder to understand the report.

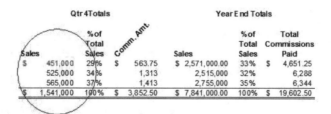

Solution:

You want the first column of the spreadsheet—the names of the sales reps—visible on the second page.

Feature: Columns to repeat at left

Step 1

While still in Print Preview:

- Click the Setup button
- Click the Sheet tab

You see that the "Columns to repeat at left" box is grayed out. It's inactive. You can't use it here. The place to access this box is through the File > Print Preview command.

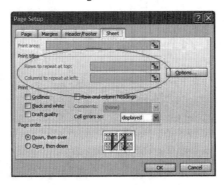

Step 2

- Close Print Preview
- Click File > Page
- Click the Sheet tab
- Click in the "Columns to repeat at left" box

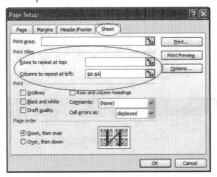

- Click in Column A of the worksheet
- Click OK

Check Print Preview to see that the sales reps' names are included on Page 2.

To add some impact to the report, you want to make the sales information available at a glance. One of the best ways to summarize data is with a chart. Charts are linked to the data that create them. Change an element of data and the chart reflects the change.

Create charts for the sales reps' sales.

Feature: The Chart Wizard

Step 1

- Select cells A12 through B14

- Click the Chart Wizard button

The Chart Wizard presents many alternatives. You choose the Clustered Column with 3D visual effect—the second chart type in the left column.

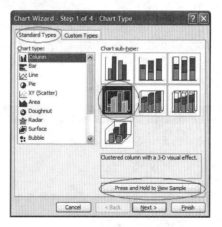

Hint:

Click the "Press and Hold to View Sample" button to preview what the chart looks like.

From your experience, you know that the simplest way to create a chart from this dialog box is to simply click the Finish button to select all the defaults. (Experiment. You can choose any number of chart styles and format any individual element of a chart. Go through the different selections available to find the type of chart you prefer and what you want to show on the chart.)

Step 2

For our purposes, simply:

- Click the Finish button and the following chart appears:

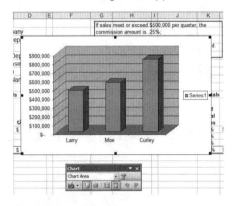

Situation:

The Chart and the Chart toolbar appear (if the Chart toolbar doesn't appear, click View > Toolbars > Chart). Also, a Chart menu item has been inserted in the menu. In its present appearance the chart is unsatisfactory. The columns in the chart for the sales are all the same color.

Solution:

Change the colors of the Sales Reps' columns.

Step 1

- Click Larry's column in the chart. All the columns are selected.
- Pause—only Larry's column is selected
- Right-click on it

- Choose Format Data Point

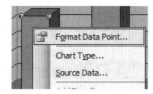

In the dialog box that appears, on the Patterns tab, choose a yellow color from the palette.

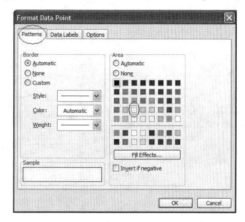

Step 2

- Use the same technique to change the color of Moe's column to green, and Curley's to blue

Note that the legend now includes the sales reps' names, identified with the colors of their columns.

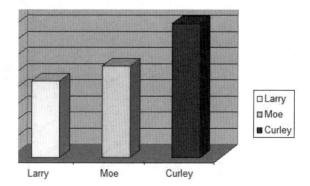

The column colors stand out better and the Legend reads properly, but the chart has no title.

Insert a Chart Title.

Step 1

- Right-click on the chart

Hint:

Be careful. Make sure that you right-click *only* on the *white area* of the chart, not one of the separate elements of the chart, because each element of a chart can be formatted individually. You know you've clicked in the correct area when the Chart Area box appears.

- Choose Chart Options

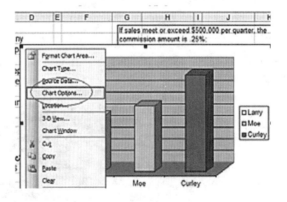

Step 2

- In the dialog box that opens, click on the Titles tab
- Click in the "Chart title" box
- Type `Qtr 1 Sales` > click OK

The title appears in the chart.

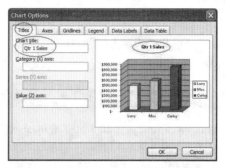

Situation:

The chart's appearance is fine, but it is too big and covers some of the data area.

Solution:

Size and move chart. (Refer to the Cursor Shapes Table in the Introduction.)

Step 1

- Click on the chart and hold until the cursor changes into a 4-headed arrow. Drag the chart so that its top left corner is at the bottom of cell B16.

Step 2

- Use the lower right-corner sizing handle to size the chart so it fits nicely under the Qtr 1 Sales area, columns B through D

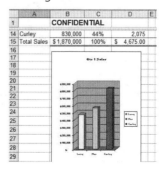

Step 3

Create, size, format and position charts for the remaining quarters and year end totals. You want the sales reps' names as well as their sales totals to appear on the chart:

- Press the CTRL key and select the sales reps' names in cells A12 through A14

- With the CTRL key held down, select the sales numbers for Quarter 2, Cells F12 through F14

- Click the Chart button as before

- Create, position and size the remaining charts

Situation:

It's been a lot of work, but you think you've finished the report. Before you print it, you want to make sure. You zoom down to 50% so you can see the entire report. The charts stand out nicely, but you notice that in the chart for Year End Totals, the total loan production numbers for the year vary only slightly, but the chart shows a large variation in the columns.

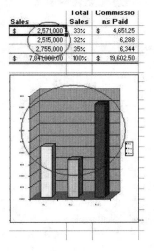

The Year End chart shows the total of all the loans, whereas the Quarter charts show only the quarter numbers. The Total Sales numbers are much larger than the individual quarter numbers. The scale of the charts is different. Because the Year End numbers are much larger, you change the axis (the numbers on the left) on the Year End chart to better demonstrate the distribution of the loan production.

Step 1

- Right-click the axis—the numbers on the left—on the Year End chart

- Choose Format Axis

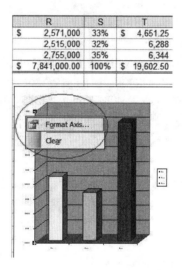

	R	S	T	
$	2,571,000	33%	$	4,651.25
	2,515,000	32%		6,288
	2,755,000	35%		6,344
$	7,841,000.00	100%	$	19,602.50

The Scale dialog box opens.

Step 2

- Click the Scale tab. After some experimenting, you decide on the following scale:

    — Change the Minimum to 400000

    — Change the Maximum to 2800000

    — Change the Major to 500000

    — Change the Minor to 250000

    — Click OK

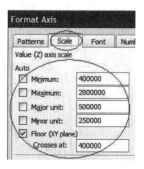

The columns now better represent the sales numbers. You name the report *My Final Commission Report.xls* and save it. You can check your results against the *Final Commission Report.xls* on the CD.

Hint:

Some consideration about confidentiality. Check with your IT department manager to see if the Microsoft® Office 2003 permission feature—Information Rights Management— is available. It can be downloaded. You can find more information about IRM at: *http://office.microsoft.com/en-us/help/HA010397891033.aspx*.

If the feature is available:

- Click File > Permission > Restrict Permission As … and follow the directions

Results

You have spent a lot of time preparing the report. A final check in Print Preview tells you that the report is satisfactory. It is well designed and has a professional appearance. It not only provides all the information requested, but the charts visually display it for easy comprehension.

Management has good information to consider. You don't know what management will conclude, but it appears that the sales reps could use an incentive to improve sales.

Your survey of the report indicates that, except for Quarter 4, the quarterly sales varied significantly by loan rep, but the YTD sales and commissions were practically the same for each rep. Loan production would improve greatly if the quarterly loan production was more consistent at the higher production levels.

You are more than satisfied with your work. You print ten copies. Because of the confidentiality issue, you insert them in a clasp envelope and hand deliver them to your boss.

Chapter Five

Create a Loan Tracking Report

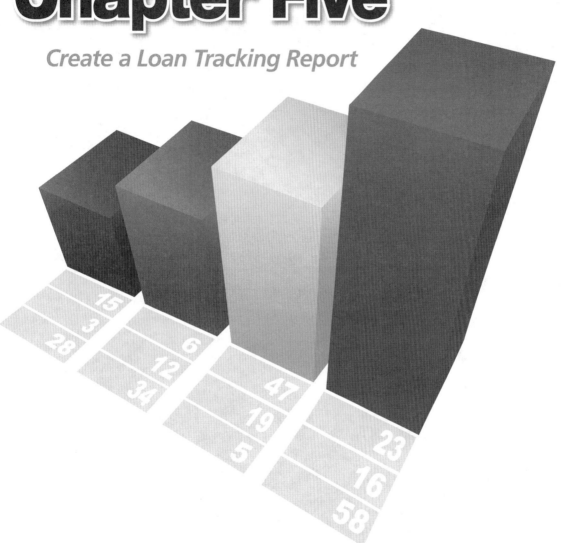

What's happening with the sale?

Your boss has been impressed, not only because of your increase in loan production, but also because you have been able to provide impressive information and reports to both him and senior management. As a result, you have been promoted to Assistant Manager.

Congratulations! In addition to a salary increase, you have additional responsibilities. You are to supervise the loan processors and loan closers. It will be your responsibility to evaluate their performance.

A primary element for any sales organization is customer satisfaction. When you were in loan production, one of the frequent complaints you heard was that it took too long for loans to close after the application was taken. This problem has to do with loan processing and closing times—now your responsibility. Although your boss didn't mention it specifically, you know it is important for you to improve the time it takes to process and close a loan. If you can accomplish this, it will be an important item to bring up in your next review.

Your best competitor closes loans on average within 40 days of application. To meet this competition, you need more information about your department's loan processing and closing times. If your company wants a good reputation, it is important that once a loan application is accepted, the processing and closing times meet borrowers' expectations and the industry norm. You decide to track the progress of loans from origination to closing, to find out where your department can improve.

Solution:

Create a Loan Tracking Report.

Feature: Database

This is a critical report. You want to find out just how well the Mortgage Loan department is doing when it comes to getting a loan approved and closed.

After some consideration, you decide on the information you want to get from the report:

- The number of days it takes for each loan processor to process a loan, from the Origination Date (OD) to the Approval Date (AP). This is the Days in Process (DIP).

- The number of days it takes for each loan closer to close the loan from the Approval Date to the Date Closed (DC). This is the Days to Close (DTC).

- The total number of days from Approval Date to Date Closed. This is the Total Days (TD).

- How efficient your loan processors are

- How efficient your loan closers are

- Which type of loan takes the shortest/longest time to process and close

- Which type of loans the loan officers are producing

- Whether the location of the property makes a difference in loan processing and closing times

The information you gather is for your information and analysis, but you intend to print the report, or different parts of the report, so you also want it to appear professional.

After some consideration, you conclude that using the data as a database rather than as a list will provide you with better information. A database is different than a list in a number of ways. A list's Filter feature segregates information—for example, how many loans each loan officer originated—but a list doesn't provide comparisons, whereas a database will. Like a list, a database's area is defined by an empty column and row.

Hint:

You can always make a database a list by going through the procedures described earlier.

You design the report as in the following figure:

	A	B	C	D	E	F	G	H	I	
	A1		fx	My Mortgage Company						
1	My Mortgage Company									
2	Real Estate Loan Department									
3	Single Family Loan Department									
4	Loan Tracking Form									
5										
6	As of:	=TODAY()								
7										
8										
9										
10	Loan Officer	Type	Pty	Last Name	First Name	Processor	OD	AP	DIP	Cl
11										

While you enjoy producing reports, you don't have the time, nor is it your responsibility, to enter data. You set up the worksheet and name it *Processing time.xls* and ask the department's administrative assistant to enter the data you have gathered. (If you want to follow along, open the file *Processing time.xls* on the accompanying CD.)

Preston,Dennis	Conv	60110	Sargent	Isolde	Ora	4/4/2008	5/12/2008	Skip	Betty	5/23/2008	Skip the
Alveraz, Jaime	Conv	60113	Cane	Robert	Ora	4/7/2008	5/19/2008	the	Diane	5/29/2008	DTC and
Gorton, Frank	FHA	60110	Sczcwic	Hazel	Sarah	4/16/2008	5/16/2008	DIP	Betty	6/1/2008	TD fields.
Preston,Dennis	VA	60108	Olson	Allan	Sarah	4/16/2008	5/24/2008	field	Diane	6/20/2008	
Quan, Mary	Conv	60114	Smith	John	Sarah	4/21/2008	5/24/2008		Betty	6/6/2008	
Bates, Kris	Conv	60122	Boughton	Gary	Sarah	4/22/2008	5/22/2008		Diane	6/2/2008	
Preston,Dennis	FHA	60115	Smith	James	Ora	4/25/2008	6/2/2008		Betty	6/16/2008	
Gorton, Frank	FHA	60113	Preston	Gerald	Ora	5/1/2008	6/8/2008		Betty	6/24/2008	
Preston,Dennis	Conv	60114	Tercan	Nate	Sarah	5/4/2008	6/6/2008		Betty	6/16/2008	
Bates, Kris	VA	60111	Wells	Gene	Ora	5/6/2008	6/16/2008		Diane	6/30/2008	
Alveraz, Maria	Conv	60112	Bell	Thomas	Sarah	5/8/2008	5/30/2008		Diane	6/14/2008	

You explain what you are doing and how she can help you. She needs only to enter the data in the appropriate cells; you will provide the formulas. She's an excellent typist, but hasn't worked with Excel® before. You demonstrate for her the various ways to input the data quickly and easily. (If you want to follow along, open the workbook *Processing time.xls* on the accompanying CD. It has the title information and field names entered.)

You have a number of options when it comes to inputting data in a database. The most obvious way is to simply type the data into the appropriate rows and cells as you normally do. You can also enter/add data using a convenient form.

Feature: Data Form

One way to enter data into a database is to use the Data Form. Once you have the spreadsheet set up:

Step 1

- Click on the cell in the database immediately under the first field header, in this case, cell A11, an empty cell

- Click Data > Form

- When you first start entering data, Excel® doesn't have enough information to bring up the Data Form. It asks you to tell it where to begin the database.

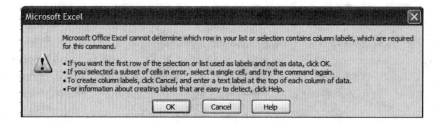

Microsoft Excel

Microsoft Office Excel cannot determine which row in your list or selection contains column labels, which are required for this command.

⚠ • If you want the first row of the selection or list used as labels and not as data, click OK.
• If you selected a subset of cells in error, select a single cell, and try the command again.
• To create column labels, click Cancel, and enter a text label at the top of each column of data.
• For information about creating labels that are easy to detect, click Help.

[OK]   [Cancel]   [Help]

Hint:

If you are adding data to an existing database, the above dialog box doesn't appear.

- Click OK to indicate that the first row is a header (label) row
- The Tracking dialog box appears

Step 2

- Type the information in the first field, Loan Officer, press the TAB key to move to the next field, Type, etc. You simply TAB past the boxes that are the result of formulas because you haven't created them yet. These are the DIP, DTC and TD boxes.
- Click the New button when the information for the record is complete
- A new form appears for the next record

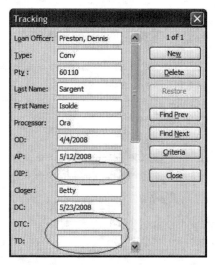

Hint:

Note the various buttons that make it easier for you to work with records.

The Data Form is easy to use, but not as efficient as inputting the data directly into the database. If you use the Data Form you have to type every word, even a word that you have already typed into a cell above, e.g., the loan officers' names, the types of loans, etc.

Type the information directly into the database.

Feature: AutoComplete

Rather than continuing to use the Data Form, now that you have the first record, you suggest that she type the data directly into the database. This way when she types a word that has already appeared in the column, AutoComplete fills in the rest of the word(s) and she can TAB to the next cell without retyping the word(s). Excel® provides the repeated word for you. Simply press the TAB key to insert the data without having to retype it and you automatically move to the next cell.

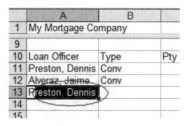

Again, when she needs to skip a cell—the DIP, DTC and TD fields—she can simply press the TAB key to skip it.

Hint:

Remember to show her how to select the range of records she estimates to enter so that by pressing the TAB key, she will automatically move back to the first cell in the range.

When there are a considerable number of records, the rows for new data will eventually be so numerous that you won't be able to see the row above that contains the Field Names. This makes it difficult to enter the data in the correct field for those records.

You demonstrate how to keep the working area on the screen. As explained in Chapter Two, Split locks the rows in place vertically, immediately above the row where you enter the command. Freeze Panes locks the rows and columns.

Features: Split screen and Freeze Panes

Step 1

Split the screen. The command is in the Window menu.

- Click Window > Split

In the figure below, notice that row numbers 11 through 19 have been hidden. You can continue to see the Field Names as you add new records in the rows below.

Reverse the command:

- Click Window > Remove Split

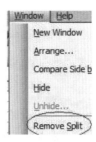

Hint:

You can also split the screen manually. At the top of the vertical scroll bar—and to the right of the horizontal scroll bar—are small, beige-colored bars. Click and drag either one to split the screen vertically or horizontally.

The Freeze Panes command works in a similar way, except that it freezes both rows and columns: rows immediately above, columns immediately to the left of the active cell. This command produces four quadrants. Depending on which quadrant the active cell is in, the screen keeps the other quadrants in view as you add more information or scroll through the records.

Step 2

- Click Window > Freeze Panes. Vertical and horizontal lines intersect at the active cell.

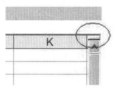

To unfreeze the panes:

- Click Window > Unfreeze Panes

Situation:

The administrative assistant has entered the data. You now have the raw data for the loans originated and closed year-to-date. You need that data to get the information you are looking for: the breakdown and totals of the times it takes to get the loans approved and closed. (If you want to follow along, open the workbook *Processing Time 2.xls* on the accompanying CD. It has the data entered.) You want to find out how long it takes to process a loan from application to approval, the Days in Process.

Solution:

Create the formulas for Days in Process (DIP):

- Click cell I11
- Create the formula "=H11-G11"
- Press ENTER

This provides a date—02/07/00—which makes no sense. You want the number of days, so you have to format the cell to show numbers.

Format the cell to show the number of days between the two dates.

Feature: Format Cells

Step 1

The active cell is still I11:

- Click Format > Cells

- Make sure the Number tab is selected

- Select Number from the list to the left

- Change the "Decimal places" to zero

- Click OK

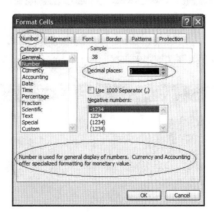

It took 38 days for the loan to be approved.

Step 2

- Copy the formula down to the appropriate cells to find the Days in Process for the remaining loans. You now have the number of days it took to process each loan from the date of application to the date of approval.

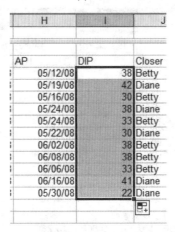

	H	I	J
	AP	DIP	Closer
	05/12/08	38	Betty
	05/19/08	42	Diane
	05/16/08	30	Betty
	05/24/08	38	Diane
	05/24/08	33	Betty
	05/22/08	30	Diane
	06/02/08	38	Betty
	06/08/08	38	Betty
	06/06/08	33	Betty
	06/16/08	41	Diane
	05/30/08	22	Diane

Situation:

You know the number of days it took to get the loans approved. You want to find out the number of days it took to close the loans after they were approved and the number of days from origination to closing.

Solution:

Create the formulas for Days to Close. To find the number of days it took to close a loan after approval (DTC):

Step 1

- Click cell L11

- Create the formula: "=K11-H11." It took 11 days to close the loan after approval.

- Copy the formula down to the appropriate cells (and format properly if necessary)

Now that you have the times for approval and closing, you need to find the total number of days it took from origination to closing (TD).

Create the formula.

- Click cell M11

- Create the formula "=I11+L11." It took 49 days for this loan to close.

- Copy the formula down to the appropriate cells

	L	M
	DTC	TD
;/23/08	11	49
;/29/08	10	52
;/01/08	16	46
;/20/08	27	65
;/06/08	13	46
;/02/08	11	41
;/16/08	14	52
;/24/08	16	54
;/16/08	10	43
;/30/08	14	55
;/14/08	15	37

You now have the information you need to manage the processing and closing process. It provides the first pieces of information you were looking for. You have the number of days it took for the loans to get approved and to close after approval, and the total number of days it took to process, approve and close the loans. This is important information, but only the first piece you need to get from the report.

It typically takes longer for FHA/VA loans to process and close (because of the need for governmental agency approval) than conventional loans. You have to take this into consideration when evaluating the processors and closers and the time it takes them to perform their jobs.

Solution:

You want to know the average amount of time it took to close the loans from the date of application. Because you also want to know the average time it takes for government loans to close versus conventional loans, you have to first sort the data by loan type.

Features: Sort and Data Subtotal

Step 1

Sort the data by loan type, to group the loans by type:

- Click cell B11

- Click the A – Z Sort Ascending button (as described earlier) to group the loans by type

	A	B
1	My Mortgage Company	
9		
10	**Loan Officer**	**Type**
11	Preston, Dennis	Conv
12	Alveraz, Jaime	Conv
13	Quan, Mary	Conv
14	Bates, Kris	Conv
15	Preston, Dennis	Conv
16	Alveraz, Maria	Conv
17	Gorton, Frank	FHA
18	Preston, Dennis	FHA
19	Gorton, Frank	FHA
20	Preston, Dennis	VA
21	Bates, Kris	VA
22		
23		

This groups the loans by type. You can now find the average time it took for them to close by type.

Step 2

Subtotal the data.

- Click on any cell within the data range
- Click Data > Subtotals

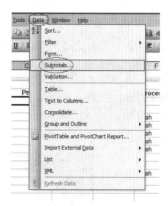

The Subtotal dialog box appears with data already in it.

Step 3

You want to find the average at each change in type:

- Click the box under "At each change in"

- From the list, choose Type

- Click the box under "Use Function"

- From the list, choose Average

- Click the box under "Add subtotal to"

- Click the boxes for DIP, DTC and TD and make sure no other choices are selected (**Note:** You may have to scroll to see all the choices)

- Click OK

Your database provided the information you wanted. (If you've followed along, your Excel® worksheet should look like the file *Average Processing Times.xls* on the accompanying CD.)

Notice that some of the column and row numbers are missing in the figure below. It was created using the Windows > Freeze Panes command.

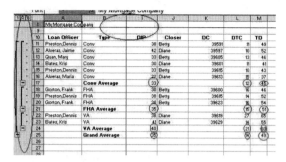

You have the average processing times for the different types of loans:

- For a conventional loan, on average it takes 33 days in process, 12 days to close and 45 total days from origination to closing

- For an FHA loan, 35 days in process, 15 to close and 51 total days (rounded up) from approval to closing

- For a VA loan, 40 days in process, 21 to close and 60 total days (rounded down) from approval to closing

- For all loan types, 35 days in process, 14 days to close and 49 days from approval to closing

This information is very useful. It takes your company 49 days to originate and close a loan; the industry standard is 45 days. Your best competitor is closing loans within 40 days of application. You'll have to improve your processing and closing times to keep up with competition.

This information also provides a base to compare to as new loans are originated and closed.

Hint:

In the figure above, the Window > Freeze Panes was used to hide columns and rows. You can also hide columns/rows another way.

To hide a column or row:

- Click on the column letter or row number you wish to hide (to hide more than one column or row, click and drag to select the number of columns or rows you want to hide)

- Right-click and select Hide

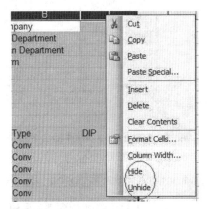

To reveal hidden columns or rows:

- Click and drag to include the column or row headers on either side of the hidden columns or rows

- Right-click

- Choose Unhide from the list

You have probably noticed something else—the left side of the worksheet has sprouted, for lack of a better word, the Subtotal Pane. It allows you to show only the information you want to show. There are times when you want to isolate information and show only that information. For example, you might want to view only VA loans. You can limit the amount of detail that appears in the database by hiding details.

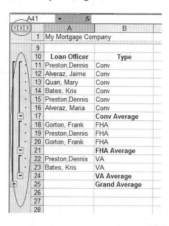

Contract the information.

An important feature of the Subtotal command is that you can contract or expand details to show only the information you want.

Features: The Subtotal pane (when you subtotal a database, the Subtotal pane appears to the left of the worksheet), hide detail boxes and contract/expand symbols

In the figure above, note the small boxes numbered 1, 2 and 3 at the top of the pane. Below Boxes 1 and 2 are contract symbols, minus signs (-). These boxes and the contract symbols below them allow you to hide detail information about the loans. (Box 3 is the default selection which shows all the data on the worksheet. There are no contract/expand symbols in this column.)

You want to show only the average times for the different types of loans, not the detail loan information.

Hide the detail information for VA loans.

Step 1

- Click on the lowest contract symbol at the bottom of the bracket under Box 2

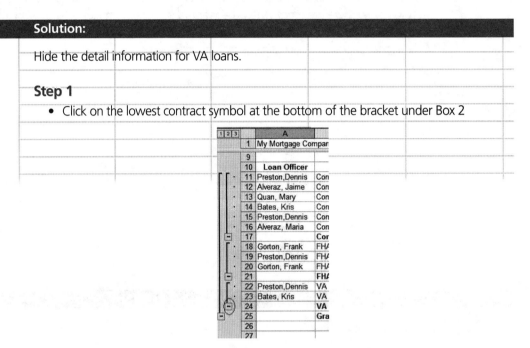

You've hidden the detail for VA loans with only the average times showing. The other loan types still show their detail. (Note that the contract symbol changed to an expand symbol, the plus sign (+). When you want to restore the detail, click it to restore the detail. Don't do it yet.)

Step 2

Hide the detail for FHA loans:

- Click the second-lowest contract symbol under Box 2 and you hide the detail for both FHA and VA loans

Step 3

Hide all loan detail and show only the Grand Averages:

- Click the highest contract symbol under Box 2 (or click Box 2 at the top of the pane) and you hide all the detail

Only the Grand Average and the Averages for each loan type show.

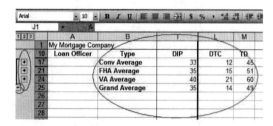

- Click on Box 1 or the minus sign under the remaining bracket, to display only the Grand Average for all the loans

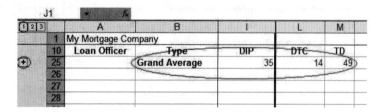

You want to see the detail information for conventional and VA loans, but not the detail for FHA loans.

Hide the FHA detail information.

Feature: The Contract button

- Click the second-last minus sign under Box 2 (it then turns to a plus sign)

- FHA loan detail is hidden. Only the averages show.

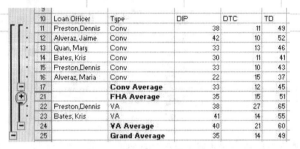

	Loan Officer	Type	DIP	DTC	TD
10	Loan Officer	Type	DIP	DTC	TD
11	Preston,Dennis	Conv	38	11	49
12	Alveraz, Jaime	Conv	42	10	52
13	Quan, Mary	Conv	33	13	46
14	Bates, Kris	Conv	30	11	41
15	Preston,Dennis	Conv	33	10	43
16	Alveraz, Maria	Conv	22	15	37
17		**Conv Average**	33	12	45
21		**FHA Average**	35	15	51
22	Preston,Dennis	VA	38	27	65
23	Bates, Kris	VA	41	14	55
24		**VA Average**	40	21	60
25		**Grand Average**	35	14	49

Hint:

This ability to show or hide detail is especially important when you want to show only details that are important in any given circumstance. For example, if you only want to discuss conventional loans, you show only those details, so the rest of the detail doesn't distract.

To reveal all the data, click on Box 3.

	A	B
1	My Mortgage Company	
11	Preston,Dennis	Conv
12	Alveraz, Jaime	Conv
13	Quan, Mary	Conv
14	Bates, Kris	Conv
15	Preston,Dennis	Conv
16	Alveraz, Maria	Conv
17		**Conv Average**
18	Gorton, Frank	FHA
19	Preston,Dennis	FHA
20	Gorton, Frank	FHA
21		**FHA Average**
22	Preston,Dennis	VA
23	Bates, Kris	VA
24		**VA Average**
25		**Grand Average**
26		
27		
28		

There's more information you want to harvest from the database. So far, you have the average processing times for the different types of loans. You also want to find out more about the loan processors and how long it takes for them to process their loans.

An important piece of information you need is how efficient the loan processors and closers are. This information will be especially useful for counseling and setting goals during reviews. You can use this information as a base to compare future times. As you add new records you will be able to see if loan processing times have improved.

Solution:

Remove the subtotals and create new ones. You do this by simply using the Subtotal command again.

Step 1

You want the total of all loans for each loan processor. With the Subtotals by Type still showing:

- Click cell F11

Step 2

- Click Data > Subtotals. The Subtotal dialog box appears.

- Click the box under "At each change in"

- Choose Processor from the list

- Click the box under "Use Function"

- Choose Average from the list

- Click the box under "Add subtotal to"

- Click DIP. (Make sure no other choices are selected. You may have to scroll to see all selections.)

- Click OK

The completed dialog box looks as follows.

You now have both the Subtotals by Type and the Days in Process for each type, as well as the total for all loans.

	A	B	F	G	H	I	
1	My Mortgage Company						
10	**Loan Officer**	**Type**	**Processor**	**OD**	**AP**	**DIP**	
11	Preston,Dennis	Conv	Ora	04/04/08	05/12/08	38	
12	Alveraz, Jaime	Conv	Ora	04/07/08	05/19/08	42	
13			Ora Average			40	
14	Quan, Mary	Conv	Sarah	04/21/08	05/24/08	33	
15	Bates, Kris	Conv	Sarah	04/22/08	05/22/08	30	
16	Preston,Dennis	Conv	Sarah	05/04/08	06/06/08	33	
17	Alveraz, Maria	Conv	Sarah	05/08/08	05/30/08	22	
18			Sarah Average			30	
19	Preston,Dennis	FHA	Ora	04/25/08	06/02/08	38	
20	Gorton, Frank	FHA	Ora	05/01/08	06/08/08	38	
21			Ora Average			38	
22	Gorton, Frank	FHA	Sarah	04/16/08	05/16/08	30	
23			Sarah Average			30	
24	Bates, Kris	VA	Ora	05/06/08	06/16/08	41	
25			Ora Average			41	
26	Preston,Dennis	VA	Sarah	04/16/08	05/24/08	38	
27			Sarah Average			38	
28			Grand Average			35	
29							

It takes Ora an average of 40 days to process her conventional loans and Sarah an average of 30 days. Ora processes her FHA loans in 38 days, Sarah in 30, etc. The department's Grand Average is 35 days. This information has many uses, from coaching individual processors to learning if the different loan types make a difference in processing times, to determining if there is a processing snag that can be cured, to seeing/analyzing the workload of each processor, etc.

Maybe Ora is taking longer to process her loans because she has more loans to process. You want to find out if the workload is distributed evenly.

Situation:

You want to count the number of loans Sarah is handling.

Solution:

Subtotal with the Count function. Because you want the total of all loans, you first have to restore the database to its original condition.

Step 1

With the active cell in the database:

- Click Data > Subtotals

- Click the Remove All button

The database is restored to its original condition.

Step 2

Subtotal the data using the Count function. The active cell is C11.

- Sort the data by processor using the steps outlined above
- Click Data > Subtotals
- Click OK
- Keep the "At each change in" box
- Change the "Use function" to Count
- Change "Add subtotal to" to DIP (and only DIP)
- Click OK

You have the number each processor has handled.

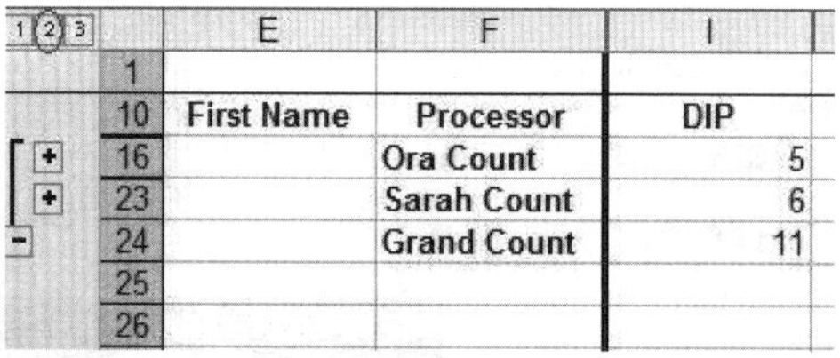

		E	F	I
	1			
	10	First Name	Processor	DIP
+	16		Ora Count	5
+	23		Sarah Count	6
-	24		Grand Count	11
	25			
	26			

Ora processed five loans and Sarah six, so it is not the number of loans that is slowing Ora down. When you discuss the information with Ora, you hide Sarah's detail, and vice versa, using the box(es) in the Subtotal pane as in the figure. You can print each processor's information separately.

You have the information you wanted about loan processing and loan processors. You want similar information about the loan closers and loan closing times.

Use the steps previously used to find out the same information about the loan closers and loan closing times. You also can find out which loans the loan officers are producing, where loans are being originated, etc.

You will use the information to counsel the processors and closers. Your boss has not asked for a report, but you know the information is important for the overall management of the department. You will eventually pass this information on to him. Make sure the worksheet is properly formatted.

A quick check with Print Preview indicates that the report flows over onto a second page. (The Next button is active and at the bottom of the screen is the message Preview: Page 1 of 2.) You want the report to be on one page.

Change Page Setup so the worksheet will print on one page.

Step 1

While still in Print Preview:

- Click the Setup button

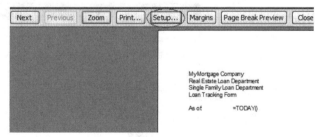

Step 2

- Make sure the Page tab is active

- Under the Orientation options, change the orientation from Portrait to Landscape

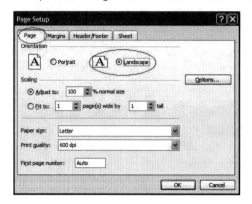

- Click OK to return to Print Preview

Hint:

A very useful feature in the Scaling area of the dialog box is the "Fit to" area. You can reduce multiple pages to one (or more than one) page using this feature. Be careful though—by reducing everything to one page, for example, the font size might shrink so far as to be unreadable.

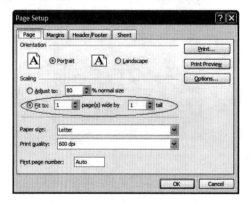

You choose to remain in Landscape orientation. Close Print Preview and save your work. (If you followed along, your worksheet should look similar to the worksheet *Final Processing Times.xls* on the accompanying CD.)

Results

It's been a lot of work, but it has paid off. You now have all the information you wanted from the report:

- The number of days it takes for each loan processor to process loans

- The number of days it takes for each loan closer to close loans

- The total number of days from Approval Date to Date Closed. This is the Total Days (TD).

- How the type of loan affects processing times

- How efficient the loan processors are

- How efficient the loan closers are

- Which type of loan takes the shortest/longest time to process and close

- Which types of loans the loan officers are producing

- Whether the location of the property makes a difference in loan processing and closing times

This will help you make decisions about your department's loan production and provide information to coach the loan processors and closers so they can improve processing and closing times.

You also have some things to consider. For example, it is possible that the number of government loans influences how fast Ora processed her loans. You make a note to analyze how loans are assigned to the processors, for both type of loan and the number of loans. Would it improve processing times to assign all government loans to one processor and all conventional loans to another? If so, would the same apply to the loan closers?

In addition to the information you needed, you also have important information about the department in general that you can pass on to your boss.

As a result of the report, you have been able to decrease both the processing and closing times. Your boss will be pleased.

Chapter Six

Create a Sales Tool

Increased sales means more work—and commissions!

Situation:

Because of your Loan Tracking Report, loan processors and closers have a much better idea of their importance in the company. They have improved loan processing and closing times. They are now close to your best competitor's times.

Your boss has used the Loan Tracking Report to review loan types and sources with the loan reps. As a result, they have increased loan production. (More things to note for your next review.)

Your boss has another request. He has asked you if there's something you can do to help the loan reps. Because they are producing more loans, they need something to help them better pre-qualify borrowers, supply alternative loan information and things of that nature—on the spot—when they need it.

In order to keep up with professional expectations, the loan reps have been issued laptop computers. Your boss mentioned that he's relying on your experience as a sales rep to come up with some good solutions.

You meet with the sales reps and ask them what tools they would like to have. After some discussion and a considerable amount of consideration on your part, it is determined that the tools that would be the most beneficial are:

- A mortgage payment calculator

- A way to compare payments for a specific loan amount at different interest rates

- A table to display mortgage payments for different loans with different variables. For example, the same loan amount and term, but with a different interest rate.

- A tool to pre-qualify a borrower

- An amortization table

Solution:

Design a workbook the loan reps can use as a sales tool, keeping in mind that you'll have to show them how to use the tools.

Your loan reps unanimously agreed that the most important tool is a mortgage payment calculator. The pocket-sized books they've been using are almost embarrassing in today's high-tech world. Since they have laptops, an Excel® workbook that easily provides the monthly payment for a loan is first on your agenda.

After some consideration you decide to design the workbook so that the different tools are on different worksheets in the same workbook, rather than have all the tools on one worksheet. This will make them more available, easier to find and use and, in general, less confusing.

For consistency, you want to have the same title information on each worksheet. Also, as the loan reps switch from worksheet to worksheet, information that is on all the worksheets should be in the same cells to make them less confusing.

Without entering the data in a worksheet, you decide on the following layout and design for the Mortgage Payment Calculator.

	A	B	C	D	E	F
1	My Mortgage Company					
2	Real Estate Loan Department					
3	Mortgage Payments					
4	Your name					
5	= TODAY()					
6						
7	Mortgage Payments					
8						
9	Amount	Term	Interest Rate	Monthly Payment	Total Payments	Interest Paid
10						

Situation:

You now have the title and layout design. You want it to be on each worksheet of a new workbook. The next step is to add the title information at the top of the all the worksheets with minimal typing. It would be nice if you could enter all the title information on all the worksheets at the same time. (If you want, open a new workbook, name it *My Sales Tool.xls* and follow along with the steps. If you don't want to go through the details of entering the title and layout, the file *Sales Tool.xls* on the accompanying CD has it already entered.)

Solution:

Enter the title and layout information on all three worksheets at the same time.

Step 1

Select all three worksheets:

- Click on the Sheet 1 tab

- Press the SHIFT key

- Click the Sheet 3 tab. This selects all three worksheets—the tabs all have a white background.

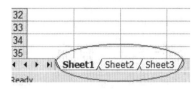

With more than one worksheet selected, with few exceptions, whatever you do on one sheet, you do on all the sheets at the same time, in the same cells.

Step 2

Make sure all three worksheets are selected:

- Click in cell A1

- Enter the title information and layout, as described above, in the appropriate cells

- Center Align and Bold row 9

- Bold the title information in cells A1 through A7

- Change the font size in cell A7 to 14 points

- Wrap the text in cells D9, E9 and F9 to better fit the width of a monthly payment

- Format cells A10, D10, E10 and F10 with Currency style to have them show dollar signs

- Format cell C10 as a percent and increase the decimals to three. You want the interest rates to show, for example, 7.125%.

- Delete the words in cell A7 on Sheet 2 and Sheet 3

If you worked on your own, your worksheet should look like the workbook *Sales Tool.xls* on the accompanying CD. If you haven't, and want to follow along from here, open it.)

Situation:

You have the title information and the layout entered. You now start creating the formulas. The monthly payment depends on three variables:

1. The amount of the mortgage

2. The interest rate

3. The length of the mortgage

Solution:

Create the Mortgage Payment Calculator.

Feature: The PMT function

Step 1

Calculate a monthly payment.

To find a mortgage payment you need to know the amount, the interest rate and the term of the loan. You've got to set up the worksheet so that the loan reps can simply type in that data to get the monthly payment.

The loan rep will enter the amount in cell A10, the term (in years) in cell B10 and the interest rate in cell C10. The worksheet will provide the monthly payment in cell D10.

To have some data to work with:

- Make sure that all three sheets are still selected

- On Sheet 1, click cell A10

- Type 250000 > Tᴀʙ

- Type 30 > Tᴀʙ

- Type 6.5% > Tᴀʙ

This brings you to cell D10, where you want the monthly payment to be.

Step 2

- With all three sheets still selected, make sure cell D10 is the active cell

- Click the *fx* button on the Formula bar

- Choose Financial in the "Or select a category" box (it may also appear in the Most Recently Used category)

- Scroll down and select the PMT function

- Click OK

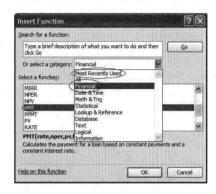

Step 3

The Function Arguments dialog box appears.

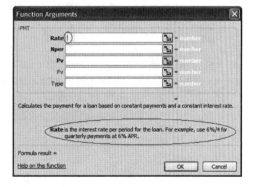

- With the cursor active in the Rate box, click on cell C10 to enter the interest rate. You have to divide this rate—the annual interest rate—by 12 to get the monthly interest rate.

- Type /12

- Press the TAB key to move to the Nper box which asks for the number of payments per loan

- Click on cell B10 to enter the number of months. The term quoted is the term in years. Because you want a monthly payment, you have to multiply this number by 12.)

- Type *12

- Press the TAB key to move to the PV box

- Type – and then click cell A10. (**Note:** This is a payment function. The payment amount will be represented as a negative number because it represents an amount to be paid out. You typed the minus sign to have the payment show as positive number.)

- Click OK

The monthly payment is $1,580.17.

	A	B	C	D	E	F
1	My Mortgage Company					
8						
9	Amount	Term	Interest Rate	Monthly Payment	Total Payments	Interest Paid
10	$250,000.00	30	6.50%	$1,580.17		
11						
12						

You now have the Mortgage Payment Calculator. Loan reps need only type in the amount, the term and the interest rate and the payment will change automatically.

From your experience, you know that related questions often occur once you have the monthly payment. A common question from potential borrowers is, "How much interest will we have to pay over the life of the loan?" Even though your loan reps haven't asked for it, this is be the place to display that information.

Show the amount of interest to be paid over the life of the loan.

Step 1

Create the formula for the amount of the total payments. You have to multiply the monthly payment by the total number of payments:

- With all three sheets still selected, make sure the active cell is E10
- Type = to start the formula
- Click cell D10 to get the monthly payment
- Type * to multiply
- Click cell B10, to get the number of years
- Type *12 to get the number of months (the formula reads: "=D10*B10*12")
- Press ENTER (you may have to adjust the column width)

The total of all 360 payments is $565,861.22.

Step 2

To find the amount of interest paid, you subtract the original loan amount from the total payments:

- Make sure the active cell is F10
- Type =
- Click cell E10 to get the total payments
- Type –
- Click cell A10 to subtract the original amount
- Press ENTER

The total amount of interest paid over 30 years is $318,861.22. Your worksheet should look like the following figure:

	A	B	C	D	E	F
1	My Mortgage Company					
8						
9	Amount	Term	Interest Rate	Monthly Payment	Total Payments	Interest Paid
10	$250,000.00	30	6.50%	$1,580.17	$568,861.22	$318,861.22
11						
12						

Situation:

You now have both the Mortgage Payment Calculator, the first tool you wanted to create, and other information that will come in handy for the loan reps. Once they enter the amount, term and interest rate, they automatically get the payment and the information you added.

The second tool requested was to be able to compare the monthly payment for the same mortgage amount and term, but for a different interest rate. This is an excellent tool to compare the savings between your company's mortgage rates and a competitor's.

Solution:

Show difference in monthly payments with various interest rates.

Step 1

Layout the cells for the comparison area.

- With all three sheets still selected, click on cell A12
- Type Compare to:
- Bold the cell and press ENTER to move to cell A13

For the comparison to be valid, the loan amount and term in the comparison should not change. You want to make sure they don't. You do this by linking the cells.

Step 2

Link cell A13 to cell A10 to keep the loan amount the same:

- With all three sheets selected, in cell A13 type =
- Click cell A10 > TAB to move to cell B13

Step 3

Link cell B13 to cell B10 to keep the term the same:

- Type =

- Click cell B10 > Tab to move to cell C13

Step 4

You need another interest rate to compare the other loan payment to. This is the rate the loan rep would enter for comparison:

- In cell C13, type 6.75%. Increase the decimals to three places (if need be) and move to cell D13.

- Now you encounter one of the elements that doesn't work on all three sheets—copying. You have to create the PMT formula again because copying doesn't work on multiple sheets at the same time. The monthly payment is $1,621.50.

- Format the cell with the Currency format (if need be)

- Move to cell E13

- Create the formula for the total payments (as above). The amount is $583,738.29.

- Format the cell with the Currency format (if need be)

- Move to cell F13

- Create the formula for the interest paid (as above). The amount is $333,738.29.

- Format the cell with the Currency format (if need be)

Step 5

Create the layout and formula to display the differences between the two loans:

- With all three sheets selected, use the Borders tool to single underline cell F13 to indicate that a total follows

- Type Savings in cell E14 and Bold the cell

- In cell F14, create the formula to subtract cell F10 from cell F13 to compare the difference in the interest paid between the two loans (=F13-F10). The savings between the two loans is $14,877.07.

- Format the cell with the Currency format and Bold the cell

- Click on Sheet 2 to deselect the three worksheets

- Check the three worksheets to confirm that the information is the same on all of them (you may have to widen some columns to make sure they are wide enough)

Your worksheet should look like the following figure. (If you followed along, your worksheet should look like the workbook *Sales Tool 1.xls* on the accompanying CD.)

	A	B	C	D	E	F
1	My Mortgage Company					
8						
9	Amount	Term	Interest Rate	Monthly Payment	Total Payments	Interest Paid
10	$ 250,000	30	6.500%	$1,580.17	$568,861.22	$318,861.22
11						
12	Compare to:					
13	$ 250,000	30	6.750%	$1,621.50	$583,738.29	$333,738.29
14					Savings	$14,877.07
15						

As the loan reps change the various elements of the loan in row 10—the amount, term and interest rate—the comparison savings is displayed. The 6.5% loan has a significant savings—$14,877.07—over the 6.75% loan. (If you followed along, your worksheet should look like the file *Sales Tool 1.xls* on the accompanying CD.)

Situation:

You have created the first two tools that the loan reps requested. The third request was for a table to show mortgage payments for the same mortgage amount, but with different interest rates.

Solution:

Create a table to show monthly payments for the same loan amount but with different rates. You'll have to create the layout area first.

Feature: A One-Input Data Table and incremental copying

A One-Input Data Table allows you to display the results of a formula with different values. In this instance, you want to display the mortgage payments for a $250,000 loan, for 30 years, at varying interest rates. Because of the nature of a Data Table, the worksheet must refer (in this layout) to the original information in row 10. (If you want to follow along, open the worksheet named *Sales Tool 1.xls* on the accompanying CD.)

Step 1

Designate the area for the table:

- Make sure all three worksheets are selected

- Click cell B16

- Type Monthly Payment Table

- Bold the cell, Center Align it and wrap the text

Step 2

Create a One-Input Data Table. First, type in the range of the interest rates. You want to list interest rates from five percent to eight percent, at increments of 1/8 of a percent (0.125).

- Click cell A18

- Type 5.00 > ENTER

- Type 5.125 in cell A19

- Press ENTER

- Select cells A18 and A19 (to use incremental copying)

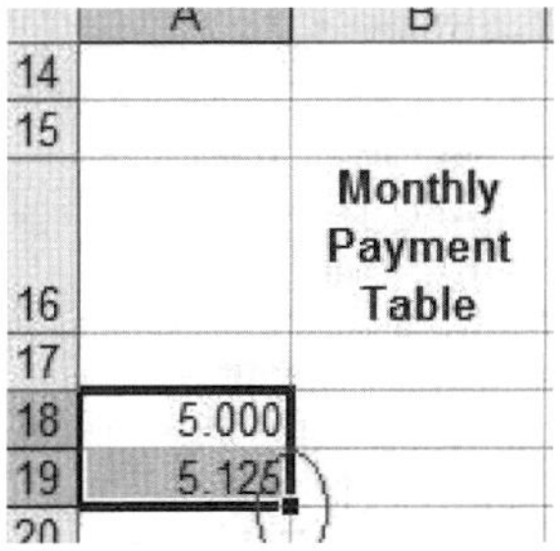

	A	B
14		
15		
16		**Monthly Payment Table**
17		
18	5.000	
19	5.125	
20		

- Use the AutoFill tool and copy down to cell A42 to input the interest rates up to 8% (when you start copying, a yellow indicator shows the changing interest rates as you copy down)

- While the cells are still selected, use the Percent Style button to format them as percentages. Make sure three decimal places show.

Step 3

Now that you have listed the interest rates, you want to list the mortgage payment to use to create the table. Refer to row 10, which has the information you need to complete the table.

- Click cell B17—create the Payment function for the mortgage described in row 10. This sets the parameters for the table (the function should read: "=-PMT(C10/12,B10*12,-A10)").

Hint:

You can type the function rather than using the Function Wizard button. The nature of a table requires that you create the function. You cannot use a link to show the formula.

Step 4

Create the monthly payments at the posted interest rates:

- Select cells A17 through B42
- Click Data > Table to bring up the Table dialog box

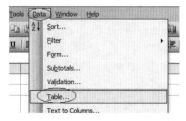

The Table dialog box appears with the cursor in the "Row input cell" box.

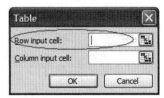

- Click the "Column input cell" area (you want to display loan payments in a column, not a row)

- Click cell C10 to select the interest rate in row 10

- Click OK

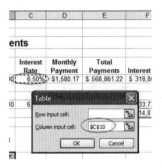

The monthly payments for a $250,000, 30-year loan at the posted interest rates are displayed. (If you followed along, your worksheet should look like *Sales Tool 2.xls* on the accompanying CD.)

		Monthly Payment Table
16		
17		$ 1,580.17
18	5.000%	$ 1,342.05
19	5.125%	$ 1,361.22
20	5.250%	$ 1,380.51
21	5.375%	$ 1,399.93
22	5.500%	$ 1,419.47
23	5.625%	$ 1,439.14
24	5.750%	$ 1,458.93
25	5.875%	$ 1,478.84
26	6.000%	$ 1,498.88
27	6.125%	$ 1,519.03
28	6.250%	$ 1,539.29
29	6.375%	$ 1,559.67
30	6.500%	$ 1,580.17
31	6.625%	$ 1,600.78
32	6.750%	$ 1,621.50
33	6.875%	$ 1,642.32
34	7.000%	$ 1,663.26
35	7.125%	$ 1,684.30
36	7.250%	$ 1,705.44
37	7.375%	$ 1,726.69
38	7.500%	$ 1,748.04
39	7.625%	$ 1,769.48
40	7.750%	$ 1,791.03
41	7.875%	$ 1,812.67
42	8.000%	$ 1,834.41

Notice the formula for cell B18: "{=TABLE(,C10)}." The C10 references the interest rate in cell C10.

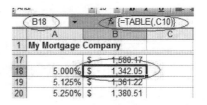

The loan rep only has to type any loan amount in cell A10, any term in cell B10 and any interest rate in cell C10. All the numbers will change to reflect the monthly payments, the comparisons, the savings and the monthly payments at various interest rates.

The next tool that was requested was a table to show the monthly payments for the same mortgage amount, but with different interest rates and different terms.

Solution:

Create a Two-Input Data Table.

Features: A Two-Input Data Table (this type of table uses two values to create the information) and select a range

By definition, a Two-Input Data Table requires two variables. In this instance they are the interest rate and the term. You have already created the One-Input Data Table which contains the interest rate variables. You have to add the second set, the terms.

You will create the Two-Input Data Table only on Sheet 2. (If you want to follow along, open the worksheet named *Sales Tool 2.xls* on the accompanying CD.)

Step 1

You only want the Two-Input Data Table to appear on Sheet 2 and Sheet 3.

- Select only Sheet 2 and Sheet 3

Step 2

You're now ready to create the Two-Input Data Table. You'll have to make a few changes to set it up properly:

- Delete the text in cell B16

- Delete the monthly payments in cells B18 through B42

- Click cell B18

- Press both the CTRL + SHIFT keys

- Press the down arrow on the keyboard

- Press DELETE

Step 3

- Move the monthly payment from cell B17 to A17

Hint:

Hover the cursor over one of the borders of cell B17 until it changes to a 4-sided arrow. Click and drag to cell A17.

Step 4

Enter the terms of the proposed loans in increments of 5 years—from 5 to 25:

- Click cell B17

- Type 5 > TAB 10, etc. to cell F17 to enter the different terms

	A	B	C	D	E	F	G
1	My Mortgage Company						
12	Compare to:						
13	$ 250,000	30	6.750%	$1,621.50	$583,738.29	$333,738.29	
14					Savings	$14,877.07	
15							
16							
17	$ 1,580.17	5	10	15	20	25	
18	5.000%						

Step 5

Create the Two-Input Data Table:

- Make sure only Sheet 2 and Sheet 3 are selected
- Select the range A17 to F42

Hint:

Click cell A17, Press the S<small>HIFT</small> key, click cell F42.

- Click Data > Table
- In the "Row input cell" box, click B10
- In the "Column input cell" box, click C10
- Click OK

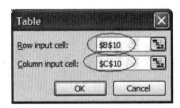

The monthly payments for a loan of $250,000, at different interest rates and for the years specified are displayed.

Step 6

Finish formatting:

- Format the monthly payments—cells B18 through F42—with the Currency style format, two decimal places. (You may have to make the columns wider to show all the payments. Check Sheet 3 as well.)
- Bold and Center row 17
- Create a header for the years
- Click cell B16
- Use the Merge and Center tool to insert the header "Years" over rows B17 through F17

You now have a table that shows the monthly mortgage payments at various interest rates and terms. The loan rep can change the Amount, Term or Interest Rate in row 10. The payments change, the savings are calculated, and the monthly payments are shown for the indicated years.

9	Amount	Term	Interest Rate	Monthly Payment	Total Payments	Interest Paid
10	$ 250,000	30	6.500%	$1,580.17	$568,861.22	$318,861.22
11						
12	Compare to:					
13	$ 250,000	30	6.750%	$1,621.50	$583,738.29	$333,738.07
14					Savings	$14,877.07
15						
16				Years		
17	$ 1,580.17	5	10	15	20	25
18		5.000% $ 4,717.81	$ 2,651.64	$ 1,976.98	$ 1,649.89	$ 1,461.48
19		5.125% $ 4,732.14	$ 2,666.94	$ 1,993.30	$ 1,667.20	$ 1,479.74
20		5.250% $ 4,746.50	$ 2,682.29	$ 2,009.69	$ 1,684.61	$ 1,498.12
21		5.375% $ 4,760.88	$ 2,697.70	$ 2,026.16	$ 1,702.12	$ 1,516.61
22		5.500% $ 4,775.29	$ 2,713.16	$ 2,042.71	$ 1,719.72	$ 1,535.22
23						

Situation:

The third was a tool to help pre-qualify borrowers. For example, if the borrowers can qualify for a monthly payment of $1,500, what loan amount, at what interest rate and term, can they afford to borrow? (If you followed along, your worksheet should look like the file *Sales Tool 3.xls*. Open it if you want to continue to follow along.)

Solution:

Create a Qualify tool. You want this tool on Sheet 3 only.

Feature: Goal Seek

Goal Seek, in your instance, is the opposite of the Payment Calculator. With Goal Seek, you know the monthly payment and the interest rate. Goal Seek finds the mortgage amount to match the payment.

For example, let's say a borrower can only afford a monthly mortgage payment of $1,500.00.

Create the formula:

- Click on Sheet 3 (make sure it is the only sheet selected)
- Click cell A7 and type: Qualify for a loan amount:
- Click cell D10
- Click Tools > Goal Seek

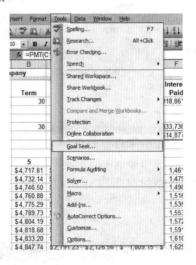

The Goal Seek dialog box opens.

- Verify that the "Set cell" box shows cell D10
- Click the "To value" box and type 1500
- Click the "By changing cell" box
- Click cell A10
- Click OK

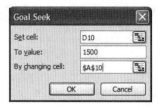

Cell A10 now shows that the borrowers can afford a mortgage amount of approximately $237,300. (If you followed along, your worksheet should look like *Sales Tool 4.xls*.)

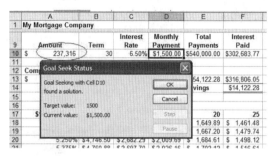

- Click OK if you're satisfied with the result

- Click Cancel to try another

Situation:

The last tool requested was for an amortization table. The monthly payment for an amortized mortgage includes both principal and interest. As you make each payment, the loan balance decreases by the amount of the principal in the monthly payment. The following payment shows an increase in the amount allocated to principal and a decrease in the interest paid.

An amortization table details the amounts of principal and interest in each monthly payment and the remaining balance of the loan after each payment is made. You could go to the trouble of creating one from scratch, which would take a considerable amount of thought, time and effort. But you don't have to. Luckily, Excel® already has prepared a Loan Amortization Table template for you to use.

Use the Amortization Table template.

Feature: Templates

A template is a file with pre-designed formatting and structure, e.g., an amortization table, waiting to be filled in. When you first open Excel®, the worksheet name is Book 1. Book 1 is actually a template.

It has a preset font—Arial—and font size—10 points. It has preset margins—1 inch top and bottom and .75 inch left and right. When you save Book 1, the Save As dialog box appears. A template requires you to save the worksheet under a different name, so the template isn't changed.

Step 1

- Click File > New

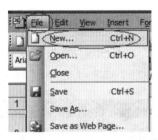

The New Workbook pane opens on the right of the screen.

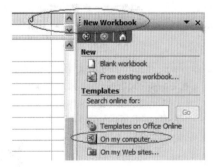

- Click "On my computer…"

The Templates dialog box opens:

- Click on the Spreadsheet Solutions tab
- Click the Loan Amortization icon
- Click OK

Hint:

Notice the other sources for templates. You can close the New Workbook pane by clicking the X in the upper right corner.

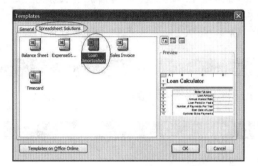

A blank Amortization Table entitled "Loan Calculator" appears. Check the Title bar: It reads "Microsoft Excel - Loan Amortization1." At the bottom, the Sheet tab reads "Amortization Table." You've accessed the amortization table template.

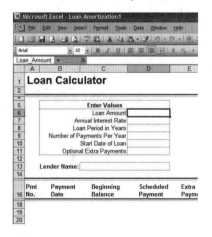

Simply enter the information in the appropriate cells. After you enter the Start Date of loan information, the amortization schedule automatically fills out.

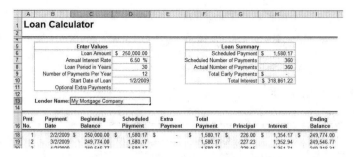

All you have to do now is include it in your workbook. You decide to create a fourth worksheet to contain the instructions for the sales reps on how to access the amortization table.

You want to create a fourth tab in your workbook.

Solution:

Insert a new worksheet.

Feature: Insert Worksheet command

Step 1

While still in the file *Sales Tool 4.xls:*

- Right-click on the Sheet 1 tab at the bottom of the worksheet

- Choose Insert from the list

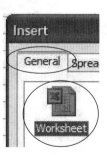

- Make sure the Worksheet icon is selected

- Click OK to insert a new worksheet

You've added a new worksheet, Sheet 4, to the left of Sheet 1, but you want it to be the fourth worksheet, not the first.

Step 2

Move the worksheet.

- Click and hold the Sheet 4 tab until an arrow appears

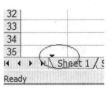

- Drag to the right of Sheet 3

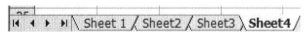

Situation:

While you're working with the sheet tabs, you decide to change their names to match the tools you placed on the different sheets.

Solution:

Name the worksheets to match the tools.

Feature: Naming worksheets

Since you're already on Sheet 4, change its name to "Amortization":

- Double-click on the Sheet 4 tab
- Type Amortization
- Press ENTER
- Double-click Sheet 1 and type: Mtg Pmt
- Double-click Sheet 2 and type: Pmt and Terms
- Double-click Sheet 3 and type: Qualify

Click on the Mtg Pmt tab and the bottom of the worksheet appears as follows:

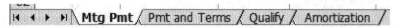

Hint:

The buttons to the left allow you to move through the various worksheets. They work like the buttons on a VCR. If you have so many worksheets in a workbook that they scroll off the screen, the buttons allow you to scroll one worksheet at a time or go to the first and last worksheet.

The default number of worksheets in a workbook is three. To change the default:

- Click Tools > Options

- Click the General tab

- Change the number of sheets in a new workbook to the number you want

- Click OK (You might want to change some other defaults while you're at it. Examine the different choices.)

Situation:

You want to have the sales reps easily create an amortization without having to go through all the steps.

Solution:

Create a macro to activate the Amortization Table template.

Feature: Macros

Macros can be very simple or complex. Microsoft® has developed VBA, a programming language. If you know that language you can *write* your macros. A much simpler macro is a recording of keystrokes that you can play back to repeat the keystrokes. This type of macro is much like a VCR recording: record the program (keystrokes) and play it back when you want to.

Step 1

Prepare the instructions for running the macro. Worksheet 4 is blank.

- Type the instructions to run the macro as follows:

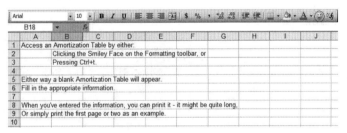

Now that you have the instructions, you have to create the macro, the "Smiley Face" and the "CTRL + t" parts of the instructions.

Step 2

Create the macro.

- Click on any cell on Sheet 4 of the *Sales Tool 4.xls* worksheet

- Click Tools > Macro > Record New Macro …

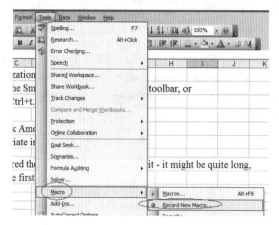

The Record Macro dialog box opens with "Macro name" showing "Macro 1." The "CTRL +" box is empty.

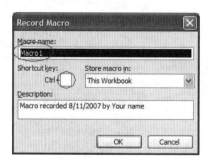

Step 3

- Click in the "Macro name" box and type Amortization

- Click the "CTRL +" box and type t

- Click OK and the macro is ready to start recording your keystrokes

Step 4

While the macro is recording, perform the keystrokes to access the Loan Amortization template—the same keystrokes used above to access and open the Amortization Table template:

- Click File > New

- Choose "On my computer" from the pane at the right

- Click the Spreadsheet Solutions tab

- Click the Loan Amortization tab

- Click OK

A blank Loan Calculator template appears.

Step 5

Turn off the macro recorder:

- Click Tools > Macro > Stop Recording

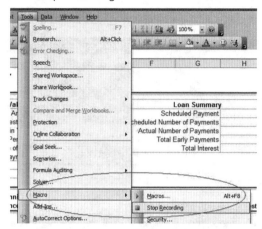

You've created the macro "Amortization." You can run the macro simply by pressing CTRL + t.

An additional feature was placing a Smiley Face button on the Formatting toolbar. You can assign a macro to a button, place it on a toolbar and run the macro simply by clicking on the button.

Solution:

Place a button on the Formatting toolbar and assign the Amortization macro to it.

Features: Customize toolbars and assign a macro to a button

Step 1

- Right-click on any toolbar

- Click Customize

The Customize dialog box appears.

Step 2

- Click the Commands tab

- Under the Categories area, scroll down and select Macros. The Commands area changes to show a Smiley Face.

- Click and drag it to the right side of the Formatting toolbar

- Click Close

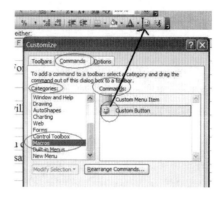

Step 3

The button is on the toolbar, and now you have to assign the Amortization macro to the Smiley Face button:

- Click the Smiley Face

The Assign Macro dialog box opens.

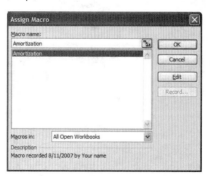

- Click the Amortization macro

- Click OK

The macro is now assigned to the Smiley Face button. All a loan rep has to do is click on it to produce the amortization table.

Situation:

After a lot of planning, work and thought, you have created a very useful sales tool for the loan reps. To make it even easier for the loan reps to use, you want to include instructions in the workbook on how to work the various tools.

Solution:

You insert instructions for the sales reps on the worksheets themselves so they can access them when they use the tools. (For your convenience, the file *Sales Tool Final.xls* already has the comments inserted and placed. If you are following along and wish to insert the comments, follow along.)

Features: Create, format and place comments

Step 1

- Right-click on cell A10

- Choose Insert Comment

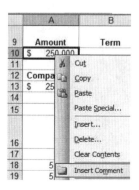

- A yellow comment box appears with the laptop owner's name in it

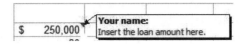

Step 2

- Type the instructions as in the figure

- Because you want this text to stand out, select the text and change the color of the font to violet

- Click the Font Color button and change it to violet

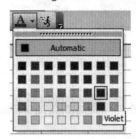

Step 3

You want to place and size the comment properly. You place a comment the same way you place a chart or graphic:

- Click the comment

- Point to a "fuzzy" border and a 4-sided arrow appears

- Drag to the location you want. An arrow points to the cell with the comment.

- Click away from the comment and the comment disappears

To indicate that a comment is attached to the cell, a red triangle appears in the upper right-hand corner.

- Hover the cursor over the cell and the comment appears; move away and it disappears. This provides a way for a loan rep to refresh his or her memory about using the tools without calling attention to the fact.

- Enter and place the comments as indicated in the figure below (Remember, the comments have already been inserted in the workbook *Final Sales Tool.xls*.)

Hint:

You can place the comment when you create it. If you want to move it later:

- Right-click on the cell

- Choose Edit Comment—point to a border and a 4-sided cursor appears

- Click and drag to the location you want

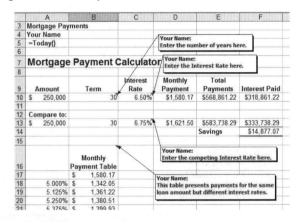

Situation:

You go through the worksheets to do any final formatting that has to be done, check column widths, etc. and finalize the workbook. For the meeting with the sales reps, you want the comments to show all the time.

Step 1

Show the comments. On any worksheet:

- Click Tools > Options
- Make sure the View tab is visible
- Click the radio button "Comment & indicator"
- Click OK

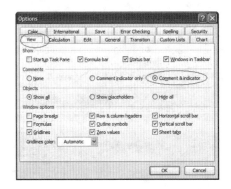

The Comments remain visible:

- Click the Pmt and Terms worksheet and enter the comments as in the following figure:

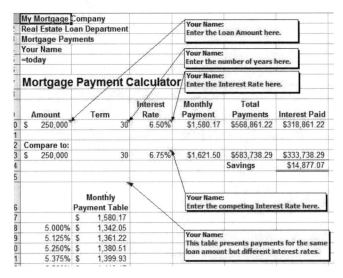

- Click on the Qualify worksheet and insert the following comment in cell B10

9	Amount	Term	Interest	Monthly Payment	Total Payments	Interest Paid
10	$ 189,853	30	6.50%	$1,200.00	$432,000.00	$242,147.02
11						
12	Your Name:					
13						
14	To find a qualifying loan amount:					
15	1. Click Cell B10 and enter the term in years.					
16	2. Click Cell C10 and enter the annual interest rate.					
17	3. Click Cell D10 and enter the affordable payment.					
18	4. Click Tools.					
19	5. Select Goal Seek.					
20	6. Verify that the Set cell: box shows Cell D10.					
21	7. Click the To value box: and type 1500.					
22	8. Click the By changing cell: box.					
23	9. Click Cell A10.					
24	10. Click OK.					

Situation:

You have spent a considerable amount of time and energy to create the formulas and functions in the worksheet. Knowing how easy it is to accidentally type over or erase a formula, you want to make sure that the loan reps can change only the cells that they need to change.

Solution:

Format cells so that the loan reps can enter information only into the cells that you want them to.

Feature: Protect a worksheet. There are two steps to the procedure:

1. Unlock the cells that you want the loan reps to enter data into

2. Protect the worksheets

Step 1

The first step is to unlock the cells that you want the loan reps to enter the data in:

- Click the Mtg Pmt worksheet
- Select A10 through C10 and also cell C13—the cells the loan reps enter data into
- Click Format > Cells > the Protection tab
- The Locked box has a checkmark in it. Click it to unlock these cells.
- Click OK

Step 2

Protect the sheet so no other cells can be affected:

- Click Tools > Protection > Protect Sheet

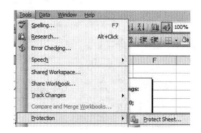

- Make sure that both the "Select locked cells" box and the "Select unlocked cells" box have a checkmark

- Click OK

Hint:

You can assign a password for extra security.

The loan reps cannot change any cell other than those you have unlocked. If any other cell is typed over, the following message appears:

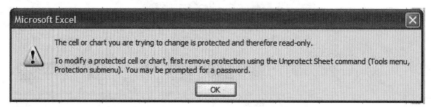

- Move to the Pmt and Terms worksheet, unlock the appropriate cells and protect that worksheet

- Move to the Qualify worksheet, unlock the appropriate cells and protect that worksheet

- Move to the Amortization worksheet cells and protect that worksheet

Hint:

Note that you can assign a password to make sure that only you can unprotect the workbook. To unprotect the worksheets, reverse the commands.

If you followed along, your worksheet should look like the workbook *Sales Tool Final.xls.* on the accompanying CD.

Results

Your sales tool is finally finished. Congratulations!

You arrange a meeting with the sales reps to demonstrate the Sales Tool workbook and prepare for the meeting.

During the meeting, you bring copies of the workbook on CDs so they can copy it onto their laptops. You explain the sales tools included in the workbook and go through the instructions a number of times to make sure the loan reps understand them. When they do, you demonstrate how to show the Comment Indicator, if they choose to hide comments.

You want to print the various worksheets in the workbook so the loan reps have a hard copy.

Print the workbook.

- Click File > Print > Entire workbook

- Click OK

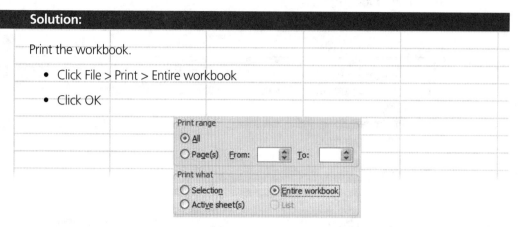

Results

You have created the tools for the loan reps and demonstrated how to use them. They now have easy and convenient ways to provide answers and help to their leads. As a result, loan production has increased. You print the worksheets for your records, show your boss the workbook and explain what you have done and how to use the tools.

Chapter Seven

Financial Statements

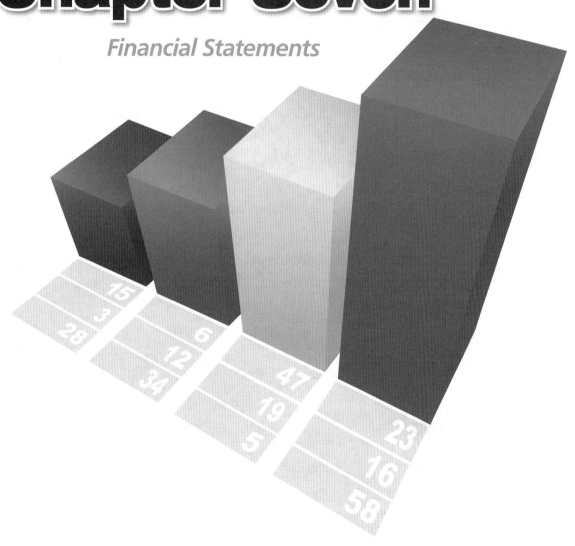

How do lenders evaluate your company?

An opening has come up in the Commercial Loan department. Your boss has been so pleased with your work that he recommended you for the position and you got it.

The Commercial Loan department makes loans based on the financial strengths of businesses, whereas the Single Family Loan department makes loans to individuals. The decision to make a business loan is more complicated than the decision to make a home loan. There are many more variables.

The decision to make a business loan depends on the financial strength of the company. One of your main responsibilities will be analyzing financial statements.

Analyzing financial statements is one thing. Coming up with the numbers to analyze them with is something different. The companies provide financial statements, the data to analyze. Making sense of that data is the commercial loan officer's responsibility.

Your first responsibility will be to provide a set of statistics that break down the financial statements to show their strengths and/or weaknesses and the comparisons of that information from year to year.

Once you have the financial report, breaking down the data is the result of simple arithmetic—usually fractions—and following the procedures step by step, something that Excel® excels at. (Pardon the pun.) Your first task is to provide the breakdown and year-to-year comparison of the Profit and Loss Statement (P & L) for the XYZ Corporation.

The specific information requested is:

- The percent of Cost of Goods Sold to Sales, the percent of each expense item to Sales, and Net Profit to Sales

- A comparison of the above from year to year in both dollar amount and percents

Design the P & L to provide the information requested.

You first need the information entered into a worksheet so you can work with the numbers. You provide the P & L to the administrative assistant and ask her to enter the numbers into an Excel® spreadsheet. She provides you with the P & L named *XYZ P&L.xls*. (It's on the accompanying CD if you want to follow along.)

A3		f_x 12/31/08	
	A	B	C
3	12/31/08		
4	(000)		
5		2008	2007
6			
7	Net sales/revenues	27778	19783
8	Cost of Goods Sold	17826	12755
9	Gross Profit	9952	7028
10	Operating Expenses (G&A)	6524	4940
11	Operating Profit (EBIT)	3428	2088
12	Interst Expense	366	70
13	Earnings before taxes	3062	2018
14	Income Tax	1071	707
15	Net Profit	1991	1311

The statement has a very simple layout. It is three columns wide. After some consideration you format the accounts in column A and insert columns and headers as in the following figure:

		2008	% of Sales	2007	%
1	XYZ Corporation				
2	Income Statement				
3	12/31/08				
4	(000)				
5		2008	% of Sales	2007	%
6					
7	Net sales/revenues	27778	100.0%	19783	
8	Cost of Goods Sold	17826	64.2%	12755	
9	Gross Profit	9952	35.8%	7028	
10	Operating Expenses (G&A)	6524	23.5%	4940	
11	Operating Profit (EBIT)	3428	12.3%	2088	
12	Interst Expense	366	1.3%	70	
13	Earnings before taxes	3062	11.0%	2018	
14	Income Tax	1071	3.9%	707	
15	Net Profit	1991	7.2%	1311	
16					

Now that you have the design, you create the formulas for the percentage of sales.

Create the formulas.

Feature: Absolute referencing

Step 1

Enter the formula for the percentage of sales for the year 2008:

- Click cell C7

- You want to divide the numbers in column B by cell B7, the total sales, to get the percent of each expense item to total sales. Because you will copy this formula down, you need to use absolute referencing. The formula in cell C7 is: "=B7/$B$7." (Remember the F4 function key!)

- Copy the formula down

- While still selected, format the cells as percents and increase the number of decimals to one (your worksheet should look like *XYZ P & L 1.xls* on the accompanying CD)

		2008	% of Sales	2007
3	12/31/2008			
4	(000)			
5		2008	% of Sales	2007
6				
7	Net sales/revenues	27778	100.0%	19783
8	Cost of Good Sold	17826	64.2%	12755
9	Gross Profit	9952	35.8%	7028
10	Operating Expenses (G&A)	6524	23.5%	4940
11	Operating Profit (EBIT)	3428	12.3%	2088
12	Interest Expense	366	1.3%	70
13	Earnings Before Taxes	3062	11.0%	2018
14	Income Tax	1071	3.9%	707
15	Net Profit	1991	7.2%	1311
16				

Step 2

Enter the formulas for the percentage of sales for the year 2007:

- Click cell E7

- You want to divide the numbers in column D by cell D7, the total sales, as before (the formula is: "=D7/$D$7")

- Copy the formula down

- While still selected, format the cells as percents and increase the number of decimals to one

		2008	% of Sales	2007	% of Sales
3	12/31/2008				
4	(000)				
5		2008	% of Sales	2007	% of Sales
6					
7	Net sales/revenues	27778	100.0%	19783	100.0%
8	Cost of Goods Sold	17826	64.2%	12755	64.5%
9	Gross Profit	9952	35.8%	7028	35.5%
10	Operating Expenses (G&A)	6524	23.5%	4940	25.0%
11	Operating Profit (EBIT)	3428	12.3%	2088	10.6%
12	Interest Expense	366	1.3%	70	0.4%
13	Earnings before taxes	3062	11.0%	2018	10.2%
14	Income Tax	1071	3.9%	707	3.6%
15	Net Profit	1991	7.2%	1311	6.6%

Step 3

Enter the formula for the $ Change:

- Click cell F7

- Subtract the numbers in column D from the numbers in column B. You want all the cell references to change (the formula is simply "=B7-D7").

- Copy the formula down

Step 4

Enter the formula for the percentage change:

- Click cell G7

- Divide the numbers in column F by the numbers in column D. You want all the cell references to change (the formula is simply "=F7/D7").

- Copy the formula down

- While the cells are still selected, format them as percents and increase the decimals to one (your file should look like the following figure and the file *XYZ 2.xls* on the accompanying CD)

	2008	% of Sales	2007	% of Sales	$ Change	% Change
3 12/31/2008						
4 (000)						
5	2008	% of Sales	2007	% of Sales	$ Change	% Change
6						
7						
8 Net sales/revenues	27778	100.0%	19783	100.0%	7,995	40.4%
9 Cost of Good Sold	17826	64.2%	12755	64.5%	5,071	39.8%
10 Gross Profit	9952	35.8%	7028	35.5%	2,924	41.6%
11 Operating Expenses (G&A)	6524	23.5%	4940	25.0%	1,584	32.1%
12 Operating Profit (EBIT)	3428	12.3%	2088	10.6%	1,340	64.2%
13 Interest Expense	366	1.3%	70	0.4%	296	422.9%
14 Earnings Before Taxes	3062	11.0%	2018	10.2%	1,044	51.7%
15 Income Tax	1071	3.9%	707	3.6%	364	51.5%
16 Net Profit	1991	7.2%	1311	6.6%	680	51.9%
17						

Situation:

You're almost finished with the report except for formatting. You format cells B8 through G8 with a single underline using the Borders tool.

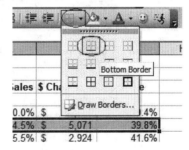

	2008	% of Sales	2007	% of Sales	$ Change	% Change
Net sales/revenues	27778	100.0%	19783	100.0%	7,995	40.4%
Cost of Good Sold	17826	64.2%	12755	64.5%	5,071	39.8%
Gross Profit	9952	35.8%	7028	35.5%	2,924	41.6%
Operating Expenses (G&A)	6524	23.5%	4940	25.0%	1,584	32.1%
Operating Profit (EBIT)	3428	12.3%	2088	10.6%	1,340	64.2%

The underline is continuous across the cells—one big underline. You want to differentiate the numbers better. You remove the formatting and start over.

Single and double underlining using accounting-format underlines. This type of underlining underlines just the number, not the cell. It also provides a larger separation between the numbers and the underlines which makes them easier to read. You have been told it is the preferred formatting.

Feature: Single and double accounting underlining.

Step 1

- Select the cells you want to have single underlines: cells B8 through G8

- Click Format > Cells

- Click the Font tab from the dialog box that opens

Step 2

- Select Single Accounting from the Underline box

- As explained in previous chapters, use the Format Painter to copy this formatting to cells B8 through G8, cells B10 through G10 and cells B14 through G14. These are the cells that indicate subtotals.

5		2008	% of Sales	2007	% of Sales	$ Change		% Change
6								
7	Net sales/revenues	27778	100.00%	19783	100.0%	$	7,995	40.4%
8	Cost of Goods Sold	17826	64.2%	12755	64.5%	$	5,071	39.8%
9	Gross Profit	9952	35.8%	7028	35.5%	$	2,924	41.6%

Step 3

Accounting formatting indicates that Grand Totals should have double accounting underlining:

- Select the cells you want to have double underlines: cells B15 through G15

- Click Format > Cells

- Click the Font tab from the dialog box that opens

- Click the Underline box and change it to Double Accounting

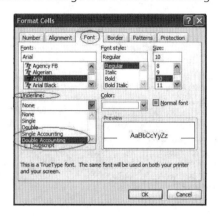

Step 4

Finish the formatting:

- Format cells B7, D7 and F7 with Currency style formatting, no decimals

- Format cells B15, D15 and F15 with Currency style formatting, no decimals, and double accounting underlines

- Insert a column to the left of column D and to the left of column E

- Right-click and make the new columns .5 characters wide

- Color D5 through D15 and G5 through G15 violet, using the Fill Color button

A quick check with Print Preview indicates that the worksheet flows over to two pages:

- Use Page Setup and the "Fit to 1 page" radio button to fit the report to one page wide

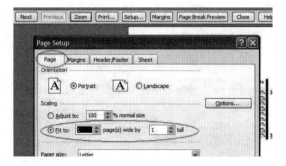

Your file should look like the following figure:

	2008	% of Sales	2007	% of Sales	$ Change	% Change
Net sales/revenues	27778	100.0%	19783	100.0%	7,995	40.4%
Cost of Good Sold	17826	64.2%	12755	64.5%	5,071	39.0%
Gross Profit	9952	35.8%	7028	35.5%	2,924	41.6%
Operating Expenses (G&A)	6524	23.5%	4940	25.0%	1,584	32.1%
Operating Profit (EBIT)	3428	12.3%	2088	10.6%	1,340	64.2%

Your worksheet should look like *XYZ P & L final.xls* on the accompanying CD.

You submit the report to your new boss who is pleased with it. The next day she hands you the Balance Sheet for the XYZ Corporation and asks you to prepare a similar report for it.

You ask the administrative assistant to enter the data into an Excel® worksheet *XYZ Balance Sheet.xls*.

	A	B	C	D	E	F	G	H
1	XYZ Corporation							
2	Balance Sheet							
3	12/31/2008							
4	(000)							
5								
6			2008	2007			2008	2007
7	Current Assets							
8		Cash	1443	1017.27		Notes Payable	658	526
9		Gov't Securities	462	131.6		Accts. payable	537	1149
10		Accts. receivable	3673	3553.2		Accrued expenses	591	855
11		Inventories	5186	7601.22		Accrued taxes	658	1315
12								
13	Total Current Assets		10764	12303.3			2444	3845
14								
15	Property and Equipment							
16		Land	548	722.484		15-yr notes	1513	1382
17		Buildings	475	550.088		10-yr notes	1316	1184
18		Equipment	1314	1667.37			2829	2566
19			2337	2939.94				
20		Depreciation	1026	1296.26				
21	Total Fixed Assets		1311	1643.68		Capital Stock	1359	1333
22						Paid -in capital	2852	2615
23						Retained earnings	5385	4053
24	Other Assets		1912	465.864				
25							9596	8001
26								
27	Total Assets		14869	14412			14869	14413
28								

It contains the Balance Sheet numbers; you create the formulas and formatting:

- Insert columns to make room for the comparisons from year to year and create the formulas

- Create the formulas to compare the difference between the years as before

- Apply the formatting as required

- Make sure the worksheet fits on one page

When you're finished, the Balance Sheet should look like the following figure. Compare your file to the file *XYZ Balance Sheet final.xls* on the accompanying CD.

				$ Increase/ Decrease	% Increase Decrease				$ Increase/ Decrease	% Increase Decrease
						XYZ Corporation				
						Balance Sheet				
						12/31/2007				
						(000)				
		2008	**2007**				**2008**	**2007**		
Current Assets						**Current Liabilities**				
	Cash	1,443	1,017	425	41.8%	Notes Payable	658	526	132	25%
	Gov't Securities	462	132	330	250.8%	Accts. payable	537	1,149	(612)	-53%
	Accts. receivable	3,673	3,553	119	3.4%	Accrued expenses	591	855	(265)	-31%
	Inventories	5,186	7,601	(2,415)	-31.8%	Accrued taxes	658	1,315	(657)	-50%
Total Current Assets		10,764	12,303	(1,540)	-12.5%	**Total Current Liabilities**	2,444	3,845	(1,402)	-36%
Property and Equipment						**Long Term Debt**				
	Land	548	722	(175)	-24.2%	15-yr notes	1,513	1,382	132	10%
	Buildings	475	550	(75)	-13.7%	10-yr notes	1,316	1,184	132	11%
	Equipment	1,314	1,667	(353)	-21.2%		2,829	2,566	263	10%
		2,337	2,940	(603)	-20.5%					
	Depreciation	1,026	1,296	(270)	-20.9%	**Shareholders Equity**				
Total Fixed Assets		1,311	1,644	(333)	-20.2%	Capital Stock	1,369	1,333	26	2%
						Paid-in capital	2,852	2,615	237	9%
						Retained earnings	5,385	4,053	1,332	33%
Other Assets		1,912	466	1,446	310.4%					
						Total Shareholders Equity	9,596	8,001	1,595	0
Total Assets		14,869	14,412	457	3.2%	**Total Liabilities & Equity**	14,869	14,413	457	3%

You submit the report to your boss. While you're discussing it, you mention that with the data you have, you could easily provide ratios for the XYZ Corporation. (A ratio is a fraction used to measure performance levels.) The data you need is already on the Balance Sheet and P & L workbooks you already created.

You discuss the ratios with your boss to find out which ones she wants. She decides on the Profitability, Working Capital, Liquidity and Debt ratios. You enter the headers into an Excel® worksheet and give some thought to the design.

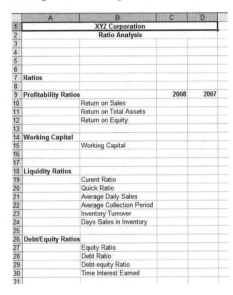

(If you want to follow along, see the worksheet *Ratios.xls* on the accompanying CD.)

You prepared the P & L and Balance Sheet on two separate workbooks because they were given to you at two different times. While you could use links to refer to the cells on those files, it would be easier to work with them if they were all in the same workbook and would group all of XYZ's information into one workbook.

Before you start creating the formulas for the ratios, you copy the *XYZ P & L Final.xls* and the *XYZ Balance Sheet final.xls* into the Ratios workbook. You copy the worksheets from one workbook to another. (If you want to follow along, make sure those worksheets, plus the *Ratios.xls* worksheet, are open.)

Step 1

Copy the P & L to the Ratios worksheet:

- Switch to the file *XYZ P & L Final.xls*

- Right-click on the Sheet 1 tab

- Choose Move or Copy …

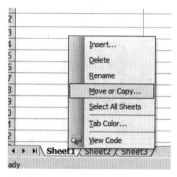

The Move or Copy dialog box opens:

- Change the "To book" box to *Ratios.xls*

- Change the "Before sheet" box to Sheet 2

- Make sure that the "Create a copy" box is checked

The *XYZ P & L Final.xls* sheet is copied into the *Ratios.xls* worksheet. Note that the inserted tab has the name Sheet 1 (2).

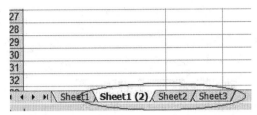

- Change the name of Sheet 1 to "Ratios"
- Change the name of Sheet 1 (2) to "P & L"

Step 2

Follow the same procedure to copy the *XYZ Balance Sheet Final.xls* to the Ratios worksheet. (If you followed along, your worksheet should look like the worksheet *Ratios 1.xls* on the accompanying CD.)

Situation:

The first ratios are the profitability ratios. These ratios measure Net Income to Sales, Total Assets to Sales and Equity to Sales. The fractions will be:

- Net Income divided by Net Sales/Revenues—Return on Sales
- Net Income divided by Total Assets—Return on Total Assets
- Net Income divided by Equity—Return on Equity

You will link the cells from the different worksheets to create the formulas.

Solution:

Create the formulas.

Step 1

The Profitability ratios. The first ratio is the Return on Sales ratio. It measures the percent profit on every dollar of sales. This amount varies considerably from industry to industry.

- Click on cell C7

- Type =

- Click the P & L tab

- Click on cell B15 (Net Profit for 2008)

- Type /

- Click cell B7 (Net Sales/revenues)

- Press ENTER (note the formula)

- Format cell B7 and the cells below it as percent with one decimal place

Step 2

The Return on Total Assets ratio measures the profit that's generated by the use of the assets the company owns. This varies greatly depending on the amount of fixed assets needed by the company:

- On the Ratios tab, click cell C11

- Type =

- Click the P & L tab

- Click on cell B15 (Net Profit for 2008)

- Press /

- Click the Balance Sheet tab

- Click cell C27 (Total Assets)

- Press ENTER

Step 3

The Return on Equity ratio. This measures the profit generated by the Shareholders Equity of the company.

- On the Ratios tab, click cell C12
- Click the P & L tab
- Click cell B15
- Type /
- Click the Balance Sheet tab
- Click cell I25, Total Shareholders Equity
- Repeat the steps similar to the above, clicking on the appropriate cells

Step 4

- Create the similar formulas for the year 2007

Situation:

Now that the Profitability ratios are complete, you move on to Working Capital and the Liquidity ratios. Working Capital indicates a company's ability to meet current debt: Current Assets minus Current Liabilities.

Solution:

Create the formula.

Step 1

- Click cell C15 on the Ratios tab
- Click the Balance Sheet tab
- Click cell C13 (Total Current Assets)
- Type –
- Click cell I13 (Total Current Liabilities)
- Press ENTER
- Click the ratios tab and change the formatting on cell C15 to Currency style, with no decimals

Step 2

You move on to the Current ratio. The Current ratio is Current Assets divided by Current Liabilities.

- Create the formula for the Current ratio. The norm for a current ratio is 200% to 100% (2:1) if a company sells inventory. This is usually referred to as a "2 to 1 ratio." A company that provides only services should have a norm of 1.5:1.

Step 3

The Quick ratio—sometimes referred to as the "Acid Test Ratio"—is Cash plus Government Securities (if a company has any) divided by Current Liabilities. This measures a company's ability to meet current liabilities with cash, cash equivalents and accounts receivable on hand. The rough rule of thumb should be 1:1.

- Click cell C20 on the Ratios tab
- Type =((note the open parenthesis symbol)
- Click the Balance Sheet tab
- Click cell C8
- Press +
- Click cell C9
- Press +
- Click cell C10
- Type) (note the close parenthesis symbol)
- Press /
- Click cell I13
- Press ENTER

Step 4

The Average Daily Sales ratio indicates the average amount of sales for the full year—365 days. (Most companies also track this on a monthly basis because they have more sales in some months than in others.) This ratio is Net Sales divided by 365.

- Click cell C21 on the Ratios tab
- Type =
- Click the P & L tab
- Click cell B7 (Net Sales/Revenues)
- Press /
- Type 365*1000 (you multiply by 1,000 because the dollars are reported in thousands of dollars)
- Press ENTER
- Change the formatting of cell C21 to Currency style, no decimals

Step 5

The Average Collection Period ratio measures the number of days it takes to collect a company's accounts receivable. When one business purchases goods or services from another, it typically has 30 days to pay the bill. This is an Account Receivable for the seller and an Account Payable for the buyer. This ratio is Accounts Receivable divided by Average Daily Sales. Receivable should be collected within 30 to 45 days.

- Click cell C22 on the Ratios tab
- Type =
- Click the Balance Sheet tab
- Click cell C10
- Press /
- Click the Ratios tab
- Click cell C21

- Type *1000 (remember, sales are reported in thousands of dollars)

- Press ENTER

- Format the cell to Currency style, no decimals

Step 6

The Inventory Turnover ratio measures the number of times a year your inventory is replaced. The Inventory Turnover ratio varies depending on the nature of the industry. For example, produce, bread—anything with an expiration date—must sell quickly or it spoils. High tech industries have to turn their inventory over quickly or it becomes outdated.

It is the Cost of Goods Sold divided by average Inventory:

- Click cell C23 on the Ratios tab

- Type =

- Click the P & L tab

- Click cell B8

- Type /((note the open parenthesis)

- Click the Balance Sheet tab

- Click cell C11

- Type +

- Click cell D11

- Type)/2 (remember you want the average inventory)

- Press ENTER

- Format the cell with the number format, no decimals

Step 7

The Days' Sales in Inventory ratio calculates how many days it would take to sell your inventory on hand at the rate inventory is turning over. This will vary depending on the nature of the inventory.

- Click cell C24 on the Ratios tab
- Type =365/
- Click cell C23
- Press ENTER
- Format the cell with the number format, no decimals

Situation:

Now that you have the Liquidity ratios, you move on to the Debt/Equity ratios.

Solution:

Create the formula.

Step 1

The Equity ratio is the amount of money the owners of the company contributed towards purchasing its Total Assets. This ratio is always easy to create. It is simply the second-last number on the Balance Sheet (Total Shareholders Equity) divided by the last number on the Balance Sheet, which is the same as Total Assets. It is expressed in a percent. Forty percent is considered healthy.

- Click cell C27 on the Ratios tab
- Type =
- Click the Balance Sheet tab
- Click cell I25
- Type /
- Click cell I27
- Press ENTER

Step 2

Once you have the Equity ratio you have the Debt ratio. Simply subtract the Equity ratio from 100% and you get the Debt ratio. (To get the Debt ratio directly, add both the Current Liabilities and Long-term Liabilities and divide that by Shareholders Equity.) 40% Equity is satisfactory, 60% Debt is satisfactory.

- Click cell C28 on the Ratios tab
- Type = 100% -
- Click cell C27
- Press Enter

Step 3

The Debt-Equity ratio measures the percent of long-term debt to equity. Long-term debt requires a constant payout of cash over a period of years. If sales fell over that time period, would the company still be able to make the payments? A ratio of about 50% is considered satisfactory.

- Click cell C29 on the Ratios tab
- Type =
- Click the Balance Sheet tab
- Click cell I18
- Type /
- Click cell C27
- Press ENTER

Step 4

The Times Interest Earned ratio measures a company's ability to make interest payments on a loan. The ratio is Operating Profit divided by the Interest Expense. The most common form of loan for a company is a "working capital loan."

The requirements for this type of loan are similar to credit cards. There's a maximum amount of money you can borrow on the card. Borrow up to the max, pay it down and you can borrow up to the max again. To handle the loan satisfactorily, all you have to do is pay the minimum monthly payment. When the card expires, assuming you have handled the loan properly, the card is automatically renewed.

The minimum monthly payment for a working capital loan is usually just the monthly interest:

- Click cell C30 on the Ratios tab

- Type =

- Click the P & L tab

- Click cell B11

- Type /

- Click cell B12

- Type *100 (you multiply by 100 because you want a number, not a percent)

- Press ENTER

Step 5

You now have the required ratios for the year 2008. Your workbook should look like *XYZ Ratios 1a.xls* on the accompanying CD.

Step 6

Create same the formulas for the year 2007 (your workbook should look like *XYZ Ratios Final.xls* on the accompanying CD).

You've finished the report. You check it to make sure all the formatting is correct. It doesn't need much because it is a working tool, but you want to make sure that the formatting it does have is correct.

You save the workbook and print a copy of each worksheet so you can discuss the information with your boss.

Results

Your boss is impressed by your work. You continue to prepare similar reports for other companies as you train for other responsibilities and hone your underwriting skills.

You have used spreadsheets to get information that has helped your company, not to mention your own advancement.

As you learn more about spreadsheets and how they can help you, you can look ahead confidently to the next step in your career.